INDIA SPEAKS TO AMERICA

India
Speaks to America

B. N. CHAKRAVARTY

The John Day Company   New York

CONTENTS

PREFACE

My first contact with Americans was with a missionary couple in a district town in Bengal, when I was a young boy of twelve. I have a very pleasant memory of the kind treatment that I received from this American couple. I met a number of American military officers during World War II in Calcutta, when it was the base of operations in Burma. I came to know Americans really well, however, during my stay in Japan in 1948–49, when I was Head of the Indian Liaison Mission and Political Adviser to the Supreme Commander for the Allied Powers. General MacArthur had taken kindly to me and to my Mission because India was one of the few countries in those days to support his policy in occupied Japan—a policy considered by some of the allied powers as much too soft. General MacArthur had impressed me by his versatility, and by his ability to talk with knowledge and confidence on so many subjects. He could talk even on Gandhian philosophy. He used to say that paradoxical as it might appear, having seen the horrors of war, he admired nonviolence as a creed. I made many friends among American officials, civil and military, employed in the Supreme Commander's Organization. It was also in Tokyo that I met for the first time a number of correspondents of American newspapers. They were generally very well informed, and some of them gave us more information than they could get from us. There were little pockets of America in different parts of Tokyo, which in those days had its Washington Heights and its Jackson Heights. I even came to know something of American drinks, my ignorance of which was and perhaps still is abysmal. Once when I heard someone order an "old-fashioned," I asked an American general who was standing next to me how that drink was prepared. He was a witty man and he said that he would describe the recipe in a manner which I would never forget in my life. He said that a European visitor on return from America had said: "The Americans are a funny lot; they drink whiskey to keep them warm; then they put some ice in it to make it cool; they put some sugar in it to make it sweet and then they put a slice of lemon in it to make it sour. Then, they say 'here's to you' and drink it themselves." That, said the general, is how an old-fashioned is concocted. As he had said, I never forgot the recipe though later I found that the slice of lemon is often replaced by a slice of orange.

I was fortunate in being stationed on the North American continent for nearly five years, without a break, first as High Commissioner for India in Canada and then as Permanent Representative of India to the United Nations. This fairly long stay gave me ample opportunities to make friends in both countries. I have found Canadians and Americans extremely friendly, hospitable and often too generous, even though they might be critical of some of our policies which they could not understand. It is that experience which gave me the idea of writing something someday to explain our policies. There are however many Americans who show a remarkably clear understanding of Indian policies and know that India is friendly toward the U.S.A. This is what President Johnson, for example, is reported to have said after his Asian tour in 1961, when he was Vice-President:

> This [U.S.] Administration is highly regarded and well received in India. . . . Mainly there is an intellectual affinity or an affinity of spirit. This, in my judgment, should be exploited not with the hope of drawing India into our sphere— which might be as unnecessary as it would be improbable— but chiefly with the hope of cementing, under Nehru, an India-U.S. friendship which would endure beyond any transition of power in India.*

Both because of its huge population and because of its past contributions to the civilization and culture of the world, India is bound to have some influence on the world again in future, for better or worse. It is true that India will take some time to shake off its stupor of the last couple of centuries and catch up with other progressive countries. Our difficulties are accentuated by the fact that we want to have a social and economic revolution so soon after our political revolution. We wish to bring about social and economic advancement in the shortest possible time—and not spread it over a long period as was the case in the West. We can do so only with adequate assistance from friendly countries. Americans, however, knew much less of India than of China or the Middle East. I have often wondered why that should have been the case. It was an American professor who explained to me that

---

* Reproduced in *The Professional: Lyndon B. Johnson* by William S. White, published by Houghton Mifflin Company. Boston, The Riverside Press, Cambridge, 1964; pages 242–243.

China was after all a neighbor of the United States across the Pacific. The Middle East again was much nearer than India, across the Atlantic. India was indeed a far cry. This may well be the reason, though I cannot help feeling that Americans might have been deterred from cultivating India too much in order not to tread on the toes of their British cousins. Be that as it may, the comparative lack of knowledge of India has now to be remedied as fast as possible.

It used to hurt my vanity when I saw so much ignorance about India among the not so well educated Americans. I was completely cured of this feeling when I happened once to watch a program on the Canadian television which showed how little Americans knew of Canada. The people specially selected for this program were those who had visited Canada at least once if not more often. No one could answer the question whether Canada was a republic or a monarchy. Few knew the name of the Prime Minister of Canada. When asked what was the capital of Canada the answer was either Montreal or Toronto! It is lack of interest that was responsible for such gross ignorance. Few Canadians would have failed to answer such broad questions about the U.S.A. because they are, as a rule, much more interested in the affairs of their great neighbor on the south.

It is necessary for me to explain here that throughout the book wherever I have used the word "American," I have intended it to mean a citizen of the United States. We in India sometimes loosely use the word American to designate all inhabitants of North America as opposed to Latin Americans. At one of the earliest dinner parties given for me by a Canadian organization I was asked whether in India Canadians are mistaken for Americans. A little mischievously, I put the counterquestion whether a Canadian is not also an American. I said that while I am an Indian, I am also an Asian.

Why should it be wrong to describe a Canadian also as an American? I even suggested that the Canadians should not have allowed the citizens of the U.S.A. to monopolize the word "American"; nor should they have allowed the British Government alone the right to use the expression, "Her Majesty's Government." After all, there is also a "Her Majesty's Government" in Canada. There was laughter all around but the question whether we in India see the distinction between Canadians and Americans was repeated. I had to admit that only the well-educated Indian can differentiate the Canadian from the American.

I have similarly used the words "China" and the "Chinese" to mean mainland China and the Communist Chinese unless the context shows otherwise. I was in China for a very brief period but I made a number of good friends there. The culture of the Chinese people impressed me most. The world would be the poorer if the great Chinese culture were to be lost forever.

I wish to make it clear that the views expressed in this book are entirely my own and do not necessarily represent the views of the Government of India. My approach to the problem has been that of an individual Indian and anything that I have said and any conclusions that I have drawn should not be taken as committing the Government of India in any way. Neither the facts nor the arguments used in the book are entirely new. They must have been used in some form or other in the past, by different people. I myself had occasion to advance many of these arguments in the speeches I delivered in different forums in Canada and the United States. They do not however seem to be so well known to many Americans. I have therefore attempted to present in a readily available form some of the material that may be useful in understanding our policies, our problems and the manner in which we are trying to approach them. I do not expect that the arguments I have advanced will convert many people to my point of view but I do hope that they may help people in understanding our way of thinking even if they cannot agree with our views. My labors will be amply rewarded if the book can in any way help to clear some of the cobwebs that have stood in the way of bringing the two largest democracies of the world together in greater friendship and understanding.

For the benefit of my Indian readers, I have also tried to remove some of the common misconceptions that prevail in India about the United States of America. It is mutual understanding that we can and should strive for. A complete identity of views is neither possible nor perhaps altogether desirable.

B. N. C.

INTRODUCTION

THE United States of America and India are the two largest democracies in the world. They have much in common. The rule of law, freedom of thought and expression, and government by consent as expressed through free elections based on universal adult franchise, are the principles to which both countries are dedicated. An independent judiciary, a free press and a strong public opinion jealously guard against any encroachment upon the fundamental rights guaranteed to the citizens in the respective constitutions. In framing their constitution, Indians have drawn liberally on the American Constitution, although they chose to adopt the Westminster type of parliamentary democracy in preference to the American presidential system of government. Liberty, equality and respect for the rights of individuals are the declared objectives of the people in both countries. Because of its larger population, India has an electorate even larger than that in the United States. Judged by the percentage of voters participating in three successive general elections, the Indian electorate, despite a large proportion of illiterates, has shown no less interest in electing its representatives than the more sophisticated American voters.

Sharing so many common aims and values, one should naturally expect the closest understanding and cooperation between the two countries. On many basic issues the relations have indeed been most friendly and cooperative. India has received generous support and assistance from the United States of America in the difficult task of building up a modern society free from poverty, disease and hunger. Disagreements and differences on certain issues have, however, arisen and are bound to arise from time to time. That is as it should be. The strength of democracy lies in the ability to permit free expression of differing views. Such differences often arise even among the best of friends and should not affect genuine friendship. They can and should be lived with. What is unfortunate, however, is that these differences have sometimes been highly exaggerated through ignorance and misunderstanding, on both sides. A hasty conclusion is reached that there is an unbridgeable gulf between the two peoples and instead of trying to understand each other's point of view, sometimes motives are imputed for no reason. For instance, the Indian policy of nonalignment was not understood. It seemed logical to conclude that since India did not agree to align itself with the U.S.A., it must be against America. Much as one may like to shut one's eyes toward such unpleasant problems, one must analyze the causes if the misunderstanding is to be removed. One must face the problem before attempting to solve it.

The ignorance and misunderstanding must no doubt be attributed partly to lack of close contact between India and

the U.S.A. in the past. Until World War II, the United States
had only limited contacts with India. Indians can perhaps
claim to know a little more about the United States than
Americans know of India. No particular credit is due to Indians for this greater knowledge, because circumstances were
somewhat in their favor. The Indian boy could get a glimpse
of American history through his reading of British history.
Because of their knowledge of the English language, it was
easy for Indians to read American books and periodicals and
know something of the people of the United States and their
way of life. Most high school students in India know of
George Washington and have read the history of the American War of Independence. They were brought up with the
traditions of Jefferson and Lincoln and they read with admiration how one of the bloodiest civil wars in history was
fought to abolish slavery. In fact, American history has often
inspired Indian leaders in their struggle for independence.
In more recent times, President Wilson's championship of
self-determination was warmly appreciated by Indian freedom
fighters. President Roosevelt's support for Indian independence, during World War II—even at the cost of irritating
Prime Minister Churchill—endeared him and the Americans
to the Indian people. During the "Quit India Movement" in
1942, when the relations between the Indians and the British
were at their worst, an American had no difficulty. He had
merely to say that he was an American and people would go
all out to be friendly with him. Americans were looked upon
as genuine friends and champions of freedom for colonial
people. Indian sentiments toward the United States were
more or less the same as those expressed by Swami Viveka-
nanda, one of the most renowned Hindu religious reformers,
when he came to Chicago to attend the Parliament of Re-

ligions in 1893. He had then paid fulsome compliments to the United States of America and had said:

"Hail Columbia, motherland of liberty! It has been given to thee, who never dipped her hand in her neighbor's blood, who never found out that the shortest way of becoming rich was by robbing one's neighbors, it has been given to thee to march at the vanguard of civilization with the flag of harmony." *

Even when the U.S.A. took over the Philippines, the Indian attitude did not change, since American policy in the Philippines was noticeably a much more liberal one than that of other colonial powers. As late as 1940, Nehru had occasion to refer to the U.S.A. as "this great democractic country which seems almost alone to keep the torch of democratic freedom alight in a world given over to violence and aggression and opportunism of the worst kind." A number of Indians who had fallen foul of the British Government in India by reason of their nationalistic activities sought refuge in the United States, which they looked upon as the land of liberty. Indian students also came to America in fair numbers for further studies. On their return home, they became the best exponents of American life and culture.

American knowledge about India seems to have been even more limited. Americans may have had some vague recollection of a thriving trade with India—a trade which virtually came to an end after the Boston Tea Party. The American-born Elihu Yale, after whom Yale University was named, was a governor of Fort St. George in Madras in the seventeenth century. No doubt there were some educated Americans who took great pains to study the philosophy and literature of ancient India. Emerson and Thoreau were among those who

* Swami Vivekananda's address at the Parliament of Religions, Chicago, on September 19, 1893.

were profoundly influenced by such studies. They, in their turn, gave inspiration to Gandhi and Nehru. Literary works of Tagore were known to most Americans interested in India. Vedanta centers established in the U.S.A. by Swami Viveka-nanda had aroused considerable interest in Indian religion and thought. There have also been eminent Indologists in some American universities. It would not, however, be wrong to say that apart from this small and elite group, there was no great popular interest in India among Americans until after World War II. Until then what little the Americans knew of India was through the writings of Kipling and of other Brit-ish writers, most of which was far from being complimentary to India. Other sources of information were the reports and writings of Christian missionaries working in India, which brought out in relief only the seamy side of Indian life—pov-erty, disease, hunger and illiteracy. The main object of their reports was to raise funds to enable them to carry on their work in India. It was believed that prospective donors would be more inclined to contribute liberally if only they knew how terrible the conditions in India were and how essential missionary activities were in that country. In this belief, American people were given a highly colored picture of In-dian society, exaggerating the existing social evils and saying nothing about the efforts that were being made to eradicate them. It was also unfortunate that while many American uni-versities provided for special courses of Middle Eastern and Far Eastern studies, arrangements for the study of Indian civi-lization and culture until recently were rare. Americans could thus know more of the Arab world, of China and of Japan than of India. This lack of knowledge has been a handicap and it is only after the independence of India, in 1947, that the two countries have been trying to get over this short-coming and to know a little more of each other.

Since then, much greater interest has been evinced in the study of Indian civilization and culture. Most American universities today provide courses of study on Indian history and Indian economics. Many more Americans now read informative books on India and there is quite a good market for such books in the U.S.A. Better opportunities are thus available for the average American to become well informed about India. Another way in which Americans are getting to know Indians is through the influx of thousands of Indian students in American colleges and universities. Indian students have always been coming to the United States in fair numbers but there has been a phenomenal increase in their number during the last decade. These students not only learn a lot about America but are also well qualified to project a balanced image of India in the United States during their stay in the country.

Even after 1947, American interest in India continued to be limited for some time longer. The main preoccupation of the U.S.A. then was to strengthen West Europe—which incidentally included the principal colonial powers—to enable it to halt any further westward advance of the Soviet Union. In their anxiety to win the goodwill of West European countries, Americans found it necessary then to go a little slow with their anticolonial policy. The image of the U.S.A. as the champion of colonial independence thus got somewhat blurred. In Asia, American policy centered around China, which was looked upon as the only dependable ally. There was apparently no place for India at this stage in the American scheme of things. In the first three years after independence, India was also far too busy with its own internal problems. The economic dislocation following the partition of India was further accentuated by mass migration of millions of refugees to and from India. India had to devote all its energy in tackling these problems.

The end of the Chinese civil war and the emergence of a Communist China necessitated a change in American policy in Asia. After the initial shock, Americans looked around for new allies. Japan, South Korea, the Philippines, Nationalist China and Thailand agreed to join the U.S.A. for the purpose of mutual defense. Americans supported the French in their fight in Indochina. India had already decided to follow a policy of nonalignment and its friendly attitude toward Communist China naturally irritated the Americans, many of whom believed Nehru to be anti-Western. Not only Indians but some Americans as well believe that this irritation was reflected in the American policy on Kashmir and in the subsequent decision to grant military aid to Pakistan. These policies in their turn aroused some resentment in India.

After World War II, West Europe lay prostrate with political and economic weakness. The United States could not revert to a policy of isolationism even if it so desired. It had to play a vital role in world affairs, not so much by choice as of necessity. The leadership of the entire Western world was, as it were, thrust on the U.S.A. In these circumstances, it is but natural for India to think of developing closer relations with the United States. Indians admire the many qualities of the American people—qualities which have made their country so great. We in India are keen to secure American assistance and cooperation in our difficult task of building up India through democratic means. The United States also cannot ignore India merely because it is militarily and economically so weak today. Despite these weaknesses, the importance of India lies in its economic potentialities and manpower, in its area and its strategic geographic location. A closer understanding of each other is therefore important not only from the point of view of these two countries but also from the point of view of world peace.

How can we bring about this mutual understanding? The first prerequisite to understanding is to try to place oneself in the circumstances of the others—their geographic location, their historical and cultural background, as also their policial and economic interests. All these circumstances will naturally vary from place to place and from people to people. Without sustained and conscious efforts, no one can adjust himself to such great differences in background. He cannot then understand the other man's point of view and is tempted to conclude that the other man is foolish or intransigent. We must realize that people will always differ in their approaches and in their way of life. We must resist the temptation to think that our ways of life are the best, that other people are stupid or wicked and that it is our duty to convert them to our way of thinking. We must recognize that it is impossible to achieve such uniformity, even if it were desirable. Human beings may be expected to react similarly only when circumstances are the same. Under different conditions and with different backgrounds, human reactions will naturally differ. The differences also often originate from a clash between conflicting political and economic interests. It is not therefore always possible to convince one another. All that we should strive for is to understand the other man's point of view and reconcile ourselves to live with such differences. That is the way of peace. Any other course can only lead to friction and conflict.

Apart from lack of adequate contact, divergence in foreign policy and differences in approach toward important issues have, more often than not, led to misunderstanding and friction between the two countries. It is not possible to eliminate all these differences. At the same time, they need not be exaggerated. Instead, the reasons for such differences should be analyzed and one should try to understand the other man's point of view even if there can be no agreement. Some of these major points of difference will now be examined.

INDIA SPEAKS TO AMERICA

NONALIGNMENT AND
PEACEFUL COEXISTENCE

FOREIGN policy of every country is imbued with some idealism but, in the ultimate analysis, its policy is determined by a consideration of what is believed to be most advantageous to it. There are of course some differences. Some countries may think only of their immediate interests without regard either to their own long-term interests or to the adverse effect that the policy may have on other countries. Others may prefer to follow a more liberal policy in their enlightened self-interest. Every country, however, has to think primarily of its own interest. India is no exception to this rule. The pursuit of peace, liberation of subject peoples, elimination of racial discrimination and furtherance of international cooperation are the objectives of all progressive nations. While the aims are the same, the methods adopted by different countries are determined largely by their own background and past conditioning. India's efforts to achieve these objectives, not through alliances with great power blocs but through an independent approach—in other words, through a policy of nonalignment—has caused a great deal of misunderstanding of India in the U.S.A. As Nehru said, in April 1963, "essentially nonalignment is freedom of action which is part of independence." We have to consider the genesis of this policy of nonalignment, how and why it came about. Divergence in the methods followed by India and the U.S.A. on certain issues, for achieving the same end results, is often due to a difference in outlook. This difference in outlook again is conditioned by our respective histories, by our geographical situation and by our economic interests. The same problem looks different from different geographical areas. A problem may appear important to one country because of geographical proximity, but it may look quite unimportant to a more distant country. History, of course, exerts a great influence in formulating foreign policy.

The foreign policy of India is a natural development of the manner in which it had carried on its struggle for independence. We won our freedom by nonviolent means which left no bitterness or resentment against our erstwhile rulers. Until our independence, the British Government conducted the foreign policy of India, such as it was, mainly on considerations of British imperial interests. Indians had no say in the matter; nor had they any responsibility in implementing the policy. We were therefore fortunate in not inheriting a legacy of past hatred or hostility. With this background, it was only natural that our general policy should be to cultivate friendly relations with all countries. We are of course more friendly with some countries than with others. For instance, we have more economic and trade relations with some countries; we have also some special ties with some of our close neighbors and with Commonwealth countries. What we try to avoid, however, is being unfriendly to any country unless that country chooses actively to pursue a hostile policy toward us.

Our religions and our traditions teach us tolerance and brotherhood. India is inhabited by people speaking many languages and professing all the religions known to the world. The very fact that all these different religions and languages have survived over thousands of years is evidence of the spirit of mutual tolerance which prevailed in the country. Peaceful coexistence of people with different views therefore comes naturally to us and is not an alien concept. One of our oldest hymns says:

> As the different streams having their sources in different places, all mingle their water in the sea, so, Oh Lord, the different paths which men take through different tendencies, various though they appear, crooked or straight, all lead to Thee.

The Bhagwat Gita, another of the Hindu scriptures, says:

> All men are struggling through paths which in the end lead to me.

The Hindu must not merely tolerate other religions but must respect each of them as his own. The edicts of Emperor Asoka dating from the third century B.C., which can still be read on huge stone pillars, call upon every person not only to respect his own faith and beliefs but also to respect the faith of those who differ from him. The idea of tolerance runs like a thread through ancient Indian history and conditions our thinking.

Our past conditioning thus did not encourage any kind of proselytization and was really in favor of a policy of nonalignment and of peaceful coexistence—a policy of live and let live. Indians firmly believe that at least in the circumstances of today, this policy is also in the best of interests of their country. This belief is not the monopoly of the ruling Congress Party but is shared by most other important political parties in India. In every foreign policy debate in the Indian Parliament, one will hear criticism of many aspects of the foreign policy but will not find any significant political group opposed to the basic policy of nonalignment. Nonalignment reflects the deep feelings of Indians, as a symbol of their independence. In view of such a strong public opinion, no government in India would find it easy to give up this policy unless of course there is some radical change in the present circumstances which is not foreseeable at present. It is naïve to assume, as many do, that this policy originated entirely with Nehru or that he forced this policy on India. Nehru no doubt gave form and content to this idea. He has of course always emphasized India's traditional policy of live and let live, as also India's understanding of diversity and capacity to synthesize conflicting cultures.

Why is a policy of nonalignment considered to be in the best interests of India? Foreign policy of a country has to be closely linked with its economic policy. While we have regained our political independence, economic independence has yet to come. On attaining independence, India inherited a weak colonial economy shattered by famine and World War II. It was further weakened by partition followed by mass migration of refugees. Economic, social and political problems had been allowed to accumulate over nearly two centuries of foreign rule. Our immediate problems today are thus problems of food, of clothing, of education and of health. We have urgently to tackle these problems as also to eradicate the social evils. Political freedom will have no meaning if it is not accompanied by rapid improvement in our economic and social life. Economic and social progress is vital if our democratic way of life is to be preserved. If no substantial progress can be achieved, a different political system such as that in China may look attractive. We are therefore passionately anxious to have a period of peace for reconstruction, for improving the social conditions of our people and for building up our economy. We have to devote all our energy to economic development and national integration. All these objectives would be defeated unless there were a long period of peace. We cannot afford at this stage to get entangled in power politics or be dragged into world conflicts. Our main stake in world affairs today is peace, to see that there is racial equality and that other countries still under colonial domination are soon set free. There can be no lasting peace so long as racialism and colonialism are not completely eliminated. Our desire for peace is thus prompted not only on moral ground but also for practical and selfish reasons. It is not enough for us to avoid war but we must exercise such influence as we have toward preventing a war. We must support peaceful coexistence since that is the only practical alternative to conflict and war.

What is nonalignment? Many people still sneer at us and say that this is a weak, neutralist and middle-of-the-road policy. It is nothing of the kind. India is not a neutral country in the sense that it is afraid to express any views at all. We are not neutral between good and evil or between right and wrong. We do not avoid responsibility, nor do we want to remain in isolation. In fact, whenever we have been asked to assume any responsibility we have done so. We participated in collective actions in Korea, Indochina, the Middle East and the Congo. We believe in international cooperation. As Nehru has said repeatedly, nonalignment is not a question of sitting on the fence; nor is it a balancing feat. It is a positive and constructive policy. If we had been really neutral, we could not have functioned in the UN. We should have then logically declined to be a member of the UN as indeed Switzerland has done. We are of course uncommitted to military blocs, but we are very much committed to certain principles, policies and objectives. Our policy is one of nonalignment and not of neutrality. There is a fundamental difference between the two. Neutrality is a concept which is more applicable during wartime—neutrality among belligerents. Neutrality in peacetime has little significance or value. The essence of a policy of nonalignment is that we retain the freedom to decide for ourselves what is best in our interest and what would promote the cause of peace. We refuse to bind ourselves in advance to any particular course of action. If in peacetime there are blocs and we declare that we are neutral, that in itself is a commitment in advance. We cannot therefore accept a fixed policy of neutrality since that would bind our hands and stand in the way of our deciding for ourselves what action would be appropriate in the particular circumstances of a case. Again, a neutral nation is one which declares that in the event of a war, it will not fight, no matter what the causes of the war may be, what issues may be at stake and who is right and who is wrong. A nonaligned country, on the other hand, does not say that it will never fight. Nehru made this quite clear when he said that "when man's liberty or peace is in danger, we cannot and shall not be neutral; neutrality then would be a betrayal of what we have fought for and stand for." * A nonaligned country may well go to war but it will not do so merely because another friendly country or a group of countries—with which it may cooperate on many issues—decide to go to war. It is not prepared to surrender its right to independent judgment on such vital issues as war or peace. If it decides to go to war, it will do so after an inde-

* Address at Columbia University, New York, October 17, 1949.

pendent assessment of the circumstances of the case—only when it is satisfied that its own national interest or the upholding of certain principles demands taking such a serious step as war. A policy of nonalignment is an assertion of independence and of the democratic right to freedom of thought and action. Neutrality or isolationism, on the other hand, stems rather from indifference.

It would be wrong to imagine, as some do, that a nonaligned country must necessarily seek to remain equidistant from rival blocs. It must choose a path different from both blocs since it would cease to be nonaligned if it sided with one bloc or the other. That argument may well be true in the case of a neutral state. The position of a nonaligned country is quite different. It will often side with one bloc or the other according as its own independent judgment dictates. It is only when it can not agree with either bloc that a nonaligned country will adopt a course different from both blocs. A nonaligned country may have opposed France when it was fighting in Algeria but the same country may support France when it advocates disengagement in Southeast Asia. There is nothing wrong in doing so. It only shows that the policy of a country on a particular occasion can be supported even though some other policies of the same country may deserve opposition.

India's desire to remain independent of power blocs also flows from a realization of its own weakness, military as well as economic. From a military point of view, we are by no means strong, and by joining one bloc or the other we would not materially affect the strength of either. Whatever may have been the military value of countries like India some years ago, there is no such value in this missile age, when the two superpowers have overkill capacity—capacity to destroy the world several times over. If we align ourselves with one bloc, we may derive some advantages such as getting some military equipment for our defense. By doing so, however, we automatically antagonize the other bloc. We give up the ideal of cultivating friendly relations with all and surrender our right of independent judgment. Alignment would not help us or even the bloc we might join. We would only cease to exercise such little influence as we have, in the cause of world peace. We know only too well how very limited is our power to influence world events. Today, the question of war or peace rests ultimately with the two superpowers. Nonaligned countries can help only by creating an area of peace and by seeking to bring the parties nearer.

There is a widespread belief in many Western countries that India has been trying to develop a "third bloc" or "third force" and aspiring to assume leadership thereof. It has never been India's aim to create such a third power bloc; least of all did we ever presume to aspire to a leadership of the nonaligned world. In the first place, it is not feasible to create an effective third bloc strong enough in a military sense, for the simple reason that all the uncommitted countries put together would be a pigmy compared to either of the two giants. Secondly, such a bloc would be undesirable since it would not serve the cause of peace. It might even lead to greater tension. It will not make the slightest difference to either of the power blocs if the so-called third bloc, comprising countries weak economically and militarily, were to join one bloc. They would in the process lose their ability even to exert moral pressure. Thirdly, a policy of nonalignment really implies that uncommitted countries cannot be aligned even with one another. It is of course right that countries with a like way of thinking on a particular issue or issues should cooperate and work together, but that does not mean that they must always agree to follow the same course, without any independent thinking. The myth that India is the leader of the nonaligned world is responsible for the blame that has often been placed on India for the acts of omission or commission by some uncommitted countries, even when India sometimes expressed its opposition to such acts. India undoubtedly occupies an important position among nonaligned countries because it was one of the earliest to adopt the policy of nonalignment. Its importance also lay in its size and population. Respect for Nehru as a world statesman was also a contributing factor but India never tried to assume leadership or to persuade any country to follow its policy. If other newly independent countries have chosen to follow a policy of nonalignment, it is not because of any persuasion by us but because their interests on a number of issues are similar to ours. Their attitude toward colonialism and racialism is the same as ours. They realize, as we do, that political freedom has little value without economic betterment and that for this purpose a long period of peace is essential. We welcome the adoption of the policy of nonalignment by so many countries, for we believe that by enlarging the area of peace, the risk of war is reduced. The very fact that so many countries whose problems are similar to ours have chosen to follow a similar policy, goes to prove the basic soundness of this policy.

The policy of nonalignment has been very much misunderstood in America. Even though the earlier attitude of contempt has changed into one of considerable respect now that so many newly emerging independent states have adopted the same policy, India still comes up for much more criticism in the U.S.A. on account of this policy. This is all the more regrettable since a number of eminent Americans have understood and appreciated this policy. It would be pertinent to quote the comments of some distinguished Americans on this subject. As early as January 12, 1950, Dean Acheson, the then

Secretary of State, said that Asians believe "that from now on they are on their own. They will make their own decisions. They will attempt to better their own lot, and on occasions they will make their own mistakes. But it will be their mistakes, and they are not going to have their mistakes dictated to them by anybody else." * Adlai Stevenson, on return from his tour of Asia in 1953, said that India and some other Asian countries "don't accept the thesis that everyone has to choose sides, that they have to be for or against us. Nor do I believe that we should press alliances on unwilling allies. After all, we had a long record of neutrality and noninvolvement ourselves, and the important thing is that such nations keep their independence and don't join hostile coalitions." ** On April 21, 1956, President Eisenhower said, "The new nations have many of the sensitivities that mark our own early years as a free nation. They are proud of their independence and quick to resent any slight to their sovereignty. Some of them are concerned to avoid involvements with other nations, as we were for many years. Certainly we American should understand and respect these points of view. We must accept the right of each nation to choose its own path to the future." †

We, in India, thought that this was indeed a correct and realistic appraisal by a great President. The acceptance of "the right of each nation to choose its own path" can hardly be reconciled with the later dictum that "if you are not with us you must be against us." Unfortunately, John Foster Dulles had other ideas. He interpreted this clear statement of the

* Remarks made before the Nations Press Club, Washington, D.C., on January 12, 1950. U. S. Department of State *Bulletin*, Vol. XXII, No. 551 (January 23, 1950), p. 111.

** The speech delivered by Adlai Stevenson in Chicago on September 15, 1953, reproduced in *The New York Times* on September 16, 1953.

† Address before the American Society of Newspaper Editors, Washington, D. C., on April 21, 1956, U. S. Department of State *Bulletin*, Vol. XXXIV, No. 879 (April 30, 1956), p. 700.

President—a toleration of nonalignment—to mean just the opposite. Dulles declared that neutrality "which pretends that a nation can best gain safety for itself by being indifferent to the fate of others" had "increasingly become an obsolete conception and except under very exceptional circumstances, it is an immoral and shortsighted conception." * Dulles not merely made this statement but went further to assert that this was precisely what President Eisenhower had intended to convey. A considerable section of the American public still looks upon nonalignment through the colored glasses of Dulles. Strangely enough, others look upon his statement as the official American judgment on nonalignment.

Indians cannot understand how the United States, of all countries, can condemn nonalignment so strongly as to describe it as even immoral. As was stated by President Eisenhower, Adlai Stevenson, and further elaborated by Chester Bowles in his book *Ambassador's Report,* the United States followed a strict policy of neutralism—isolationism—for well over a century. Indians therefore least expected Americans to criticize their policy in such strong terms. One has only to read George Washington's Farewell Address in 1796, to understand that his advice to his compatriots was equally applicable to Indians when they attained independence in 1947. The United States had just emerged from colonial rule. It had little military strength but had some moral influence. It had tremendous internal problems, economic and political, to handle. It had to devote all its energies to national integration and consolidation. These were exactly the circumstances which confronted India—perhaps in an even more acute form. Within a few years of achieving independence, the United States faced a world—which then virtually meant Europe—

* Address at Iowa College on June 9, 1956, U. S. Department of State *Bulletin*, Vol. XXXIV, No. 886 (June 18, 1956), pp. 999–1000.

sharply divided into two opposing blocs. Revolutionary France was fighting a European coalition and this fighting went on, with short breaks, for the entire period between 1793 and 1815. India, on her independence, also faced two strong power blocs dividing the world. Like the United States, India too found it natural for a young nation to avoid foreign entanglements at a time when it had to direct all its energy to its own development and consolidation. Alliances with power blocs had been viewed with distaste by the United States just as India does now. India tries to avoid getting involved in great power conflicts just as the U.S.A. did until it became a great power itself.

It would be interesting to quote some relevant extracts from Washington's Farewell Address which laid the cornerstone of American foreign policy for nearly a century and a half. Washington advised his countrymen to "observe good faith and justice toward all nations; cultivate peace and harmony with all," and to exclude "permanent inveterate antipathies against particular nations and passionate attachment for others." "The nation which indulges toward another an habitual hatred, or an habitual fondness, is in some degree a slave. It is a slave to its animosity or to its affection, either of which is sufficient to lead it astray from its duty and its interest. . . . Europe has a set of primary interests which to us have none or a very remote relation. Hence she must be engaged in frequent controversies, the causes of which are essentially foreign to our concerns. Hence therefore it must be unwise in us to implicate ourselves, by artificial ties, in the ordinary vicissitudes of her politics, or the ordinary combinations and collisions of her friendships, or enmities." "Our detached and distant situation invites and enables us to pursue a different course. . . . Why by interweaving our destiny with that of any part of Europe, entangle our peace and prosperity in the toils of European ambition, rivalship, interest, humor or caprice? It is our true policy to steer clear of permanent alliances with any portion of the foreign world." Washington expressed his conviction that "if we remain one people under an efficient government the period is not far off . . . when we may choose peace or war as our interest guided by our justice shall counsel." Jefferson was only re-emphasizing this policy when in his first inaugural address on March 4, 1801, he advocated "peace, commerce and honest friendship with all nations—entangling alliances with none."

The Indian policy of nonalignment is quite in keeping with these sound pieces of advice; e.g., no enmity toward anyone, no involvement in other people's quarrels, no alignment with blocs, no entanglement with military alliances and no surrender of judgment. There is certainly an analogy and the advice has a bearing in so far as it shows that this is a natural policy for a newly independent country. Many Americans, on the other hand, argue that the analogy is more apparent than real. For one thing, the world today is quite different from the world of 1796 which Washington knew. What he said might have been sound in the circumstances then but cannot be correct in the circumstances of the contemporary world. Secondly, it is argued that the great struggle for power and the conflicting ideologies that characterize the world of today had no parallel in the days of Washington. Nobody denies these differences. It is no one's thesis that the conditions have remained exactly the same during all the years that have elapsed since Washington spoke. The "detached and distant situation" that he spoke about certainly no longer obtains in the world of today. But then it should not be forgotten that the policy that Washington followed during his tenure as President, the policy that he advised his compatriots in 1796 to adopt, was precisely the policy that successive

American governments followed for close on a century and a half. The policy of isolationism was not given up in consideration of the changes that were taking place in the world. It continued, with a brief interlude during World War I, right up to the Japanese attack on Pearl Harbor in December 1941. When World War I broke out, President Wilson immediately issued a proclamation of neutrality. The European conflict seemed of little concern to the Americans, who were still bent on a policy of isolation. The violation of Belgian neutrality by the Imperial German Government with cynical contempt as "a scrap of paper" did not evoke any condemnation from the U.S. Government although many individual Americans felt that there was a moral obligation to denounce such gross violation of international law. No single factor compelled the Americans to join the war at a later date on the side of the Allies. British propaganda, American sympathy for and economic ties with the Allies, all helped but unrestricted submarine warfare by the Germans was undoubtedly the immediate cause of American entry in the war. Isolationism was given up only when American economy and financial interests were threatened and American lives were lost as a result of the submarine warfare. Soon after the end of the war, Americans went back again to the policy of isolation.

This desire to go back to isolationism was partly responsible for the refusal of the United States Senate to ratify the peace treaty and preventing the United States from becoming a member of the League of Nations. It was President Wilson who had insisted on the covenant of the League of Nations being made an integral part of the Treaty of Versailles. American public opinion was once again firmly set against foreign entanglement. From 1935 to 1937 this public opinion found expression in a series of Neutrality Acts, the object of which was to keep the United States out of future wars. Even in World War II, Americans remained neutral as long as possible. Once again, despite sympathy with the British, despite American repugnance to Nazism and Fascism, America stuck to its policy of isolationism until it was actually attacked. If, after the fall of France, Britain had surrendered, the war would have come to an end with complete victory for the Axis Powers. Even this real danger did not induce America to join the war on the side of Britain. It required the surprise attack on Pearl Harbor to shake the Americans out of their isolationism.

By 1941, the world had certainly changed a lot since the days of Washington. The world had certainly come much closer together by then. Yet the policy of isolationism advised by Washington continued even though the "detached and distant situation" had changed. The argument that the circumstances have changed since the days of Washington does not thus seem to have prevented American policy makers from adhering to isolationism. In fact, it is only after World War II that circumstances forced Americans to abandon isolationism. They had no alternative but to accept the responsibility that was thrust upon them, when they emerged as one of the two superpowers, and had to assume the leadership of the Western world. No other power was strong enough to lead, for both Britain and France had come out of war much too weak to lead.

The struggle for power between Napoleonic France and England must have been a great struggle in those days. There was also then a conflict in ideology between republican France and royalist England and her allies. Republicanism was not then looked upon with favor. It is true that the stakes today are higher and the danger to the world is much greater but then the difference is only one of degree. Paradoxical as it may seem, the risk of a world war is perhaps much less today precisely because of the realization that the stakes are much higher and that an all-out war today would be disastrous. A war between the rival blocs has to be ruled out because of the balance of nuclear terror. Neither party is likely to use nuclear weapons because of the danger of instant retaliation. What can then be the point in small powers lining up with one or the other bloc? It would make no difference since, in the final analysis, the responsibility of war or peace rests today on the two superpowers. The small powers can only have marginal and some moral influence which they can exercise in and out of the United Nations. The argument for lining up was, if at all, much stronger in the days of Washington. In 1793 or 1815 American alliance with either France or with England might have tilted the balance in favor of one or the other rival power. An alliance in those circumstances might even have prevented a war. It is more than possible that World War I or World War II might have been avoided if the United States, which was then undoubtedly a strong power, had unequivocally announced its attention of joining the Allies. If Americans can justify maintaining their neutrality even under those circumstances, surely they should not condemn the policy of nonalignment today when alliance of small powers with either bloc has little or no value. They can at least collectively exert much more moral pressure now in the UN than the U.S.A. could do by itself at a time when there was no such world forum; surely it should not grudge the newly independent countries some reasonable period of time to tackle their grave internal problems with all their energy. The analogy may not be altogether perfect but is close enough and it explains why so many newly independent countries are emotionally attracted to the policy of nonalignment.

One would have thought that the policy of nonalignment should please Americans at least, as it was based on the wise policy that was laid down by Washington and was followed by Americans themselves right up to 1941. Indians were therefore pained when Dulles declared that the policy of nonalignment is not only shortsighted but is immoral. Whether a nonaligned country would ultimately remain neutral in the event of a war, irrespective of the issues at stake, is yet to be tested. If, however, a refusal to align oneself with either bloc in a Cold War is to be considered immoral, one cannot help asking how the American neutrality in the initial stages of both the first and second World Wars could be justified. Even though great issues—and moral ones at that—were at stake, the United States did not join these wars until it was forced to do so in defense of its own national interests. Why then should a nonaligned country be required to line up with a bloc and surrender its judgment in advance? Americans seem to believe that if a country is not aligned with them it must be against them. Does this lining up help the United States in any way? Americans should be satisfied if a country is not positively aligned against them. The best contribution that small or militarily weak countries can make toward peace is to develop enough strength, military and economic, to defend themselves and maintain their independence. By doing so, they at least extend the area of democratic freedom and at least indirectly strengthen the free world.

The Dullesian views on nonalignment which unfortunately prevailed in America, over the more tolerant views of others, have done a lot of harm to the cause of Indo-American understanding. India, being one of the first countries to adopt a policy of nonalignment, naturally became the principal target of attack. Even when many other newly independent countries chose to adopt the same policy, India was blamed for having shown them the way by its own example! It was not appreciated that these countries would have evolved the same policy, in their own interest, irrespective of what India did. The newly emerging independent countries were determined to think for themselves and take their own decisions. American criticism against it did not dissuade them from adopting a policy of nonalignment. The only effect of such criticism was to alienate their sympathy. Americans condemned nonalignment although, as a democracy, they were expected to welcome independent thinking, which is what nonaligned countries claim as their right. The Soviet Union also began by condemning nonalignment. During the first few years of our independence, it too was suspicious and critical of nonalignment. Nonaligned India's decision to remain in the Commonwealth merely confirmed its belief that it was a stooge of British imperialism. Gradually, the realization came that nonalignment was a symbol of nationalism and a firm assertion of independence. The Soviet Union saw the danger of moving against this strong tide of nationalism and made peace with nonalignment. It was content to let these countries remain nonaligned so long as they did not join the Western bloc. In doing so, it appeared to show its tolerance for nonalignment. Americans, perhaps unwittingly, left the field clear for the Russians to cultivate the nonaligned world. By joining forces with the nonaligned countries in their fight against racialism and Western colonialism, the Soviet Union gave the impression of being more friendly toward causes dear to the erstwhile colonial peoples. The main argument against totalitarianism, that it is opposed to any individual freedom as well as freedom of thought and speech, lost much of its force when, in the international sphere, totalitarianism appeared in practice to be more tolerant of other peoples' views. A much more sympathetic understanding of nonalignment in America in recent years has not yet been able entirely to undo the harm that had been caused in the past. The inability to understand the implications and the causes of nonalignment may well be considered by future historians as a grave failure of postwar American foreign policy. Americans failed to appreciate why the newly independent countries were not prepared to surrender any part of their sovereignty by aligning themselves with the Western bloc, particularly when so many older countries agreed to do so, in mutual interest. It should have been appreciated that some time must elapse before the newly independent countries can be expected to forget the days of colonial rule and agree to surrender their judgment to a bloc which includes all the past or present colonial powers. This refusal to line up with the West should not have given rise to the suspicion as if the nonaligned countries were Communists or pseudo Communists. On the contrary, the majority of these countries are in fact preponderantly Western-oriented, at least culturally and economically if not quite so much politically.

A question that has often been asked is why even after the Chinese attack of 1962, India continued to follow a policy of nonalignment. After the prompt and unconditional response of the U.S.A. and some other Western powers to Prime Minister Nehru's appeal for help, one would have expected India to know who its friends were and to change its policy accordingly. In the wake of the Chinese attack and ever since then, there has indeed been a substantial volume of public opinion in India demanding an abandonment of the policy of nonalignment and supporting instead an alliance with the Western bloc, for defensive purposes. According to this school of thought, the invasion by China clearly proved the unreliability of so-called friends from the Communist world. Communists as a rule are treacherous, so ran the argument, and as such India should align itself with its friends in the West. Prime Minister Nehru on the other hand strongly held the view that the Chinese invasion had nothing to do with Communism as such. It was the result of a policy of aggressive expansionism which a strong and militant China had adopted. Communism might have helped in the building up of a united, intensely nationalistic and militant China but once there was such a buildup, China would have invaded India, irrespective of the nature of government actually in power in China. It was therefore wrong to assume that a non-Communist but a militant China would never have attacked India. If any "ism" is responsible for this attack it is aggressive nationalism or expansionism. Despite this sound reasoning, even Prime Minister Nehru would perhaps have found it difficult to hold on to a policy of nonalignment in the face of mounting pressure of public opinion. Because of the prompt and generous response from the U.S.A. and friendly Western countries, there was a wave of goodwill in India for these countries and there was a strong demand from a large section of the people for a defensive alliance with the West. This fund of goodwill, however, dried up and the demand became weaker, when an unfortunate attempt was made to tie up further military assistance from the West with the question of a settlement of the Kashmir problem. The attempt was a well-meaning one, since it was generally acknowledged that Indo-Pakistan amity would make defense against China much easier. The method followed however was foredoomed to failure. If instead of merely creating an impression that further military aid to India would be contingent on India's trying to settle the Kashmir question with Pakistan, pressure had been put on both India and Pakistan to come to some agreement and Pakistan had been told that military aid to Pakistan was also contingent on such an agreement, there might have been some chance of success.

The refusal of Indian requests for supersonic aircraft, heavy tanks and submarines, all of which had been given to Pakistan, only confirmed the Pakistani belief that it could exercise some sort of a veto on the further flow of military aid to India from the West. The result was that Pakistan became completely rigid and intransigent. The announcement that there has been an agreement in principle with China in respect of the borders of the Pakistani-held portion of Kashmir was made to coincide exactly with the opening of the Indo-Pakistani talks on Kashmir in December 1962. This was an act of extreme provocation and was perhaps intended to make India break off the talks. Even so, India decided to carry on the talks. The formal agreement with China on this border was signed by the Foreign Minister of Pakistan in March 1963, when the talks on Kashmir were still going on. India, however, continued the talks until Pakistan broke off the talks in June 1963, after making it clear that there could be no settlement except on its own terms. Open Pakistani support for China on the Sino-Indian dispute and virulent anti-Indian propaganda in Pakistan made it impossible to create a climate for fruitful talks.

Western pressure on India, by creating an impression that military aid might be contingent on a settlement of the Kashmir question, thus not only did not produce any tangible result but also led to the loss of much of the goodwill that had been created as a result of the prompt assistance received from the West. Doubts began to be raised about the advisability of giving up the policy of nonalignment, particularly when in the meantime the Soviet Union and most socialist countries came out more openly in favor of India in the Sino-Indian conflict. With the Sino-Soviet dispute becoming more acute,

India actually received promises of military hardware from the Soviet Union on favorable terms of payment. It confirmed Prime Minister Nehru's views—if a confirmation was at all needed—that the Chinese attack on India had nothing to do with the Communist ideology. The Soviet Union would have hardly assisted India if the Chinese attack had been in furtherance of the interests of international Communism. The fact that the Soviet Union was prepared to supply certain sophisticated military equipment which had been refused by the U.S.A., out of deference to the wishes of Pakistan, made the USSR all the more popular. In the circumstances, the question of giving up the policy of nonalignment could no longer be seriously considered.

While this development may superficially appear to be against American interests, it is really not so. If after the Chinese invasion, India had decided to seek military alliance with its Western friends, the Sino-Indian conflict would have become a Cold War issue. That is exactly what China had expected. For some time, it looked as if India had no alternative but to abandon its cherished policy of nonalignment. It was a great disappointment to China that this did not happen and that its well-conceived plan to make the conflict a Cold War issue did not succeed. The United States and the United Kingdom deserve great credit for the farsightedness shown by them in not even suggesting to India that it should give up its basic policy of nonalignment. The prompt and unconditional nature of the assistance was appreciated in India even more than the quantum of the military aid. The failure of the Chinese plan to make the Sino-Indian conflict a Cold War issue has not only been of benefit to India but also to our Western friends, who were saved from the embarrassment of getting involved in this conflict and entering into a commitment to defend India. That would indeed have been the case had India sought military alliance with the West. The military aid received from friendly countries is helping India to build up its own defensive capacity. The danger of local conflict escalating into a third world war has been eliminated. India's continued adherence to the policy of nonalignment, even after the Chinese attack, may have been a disappointment for the Chinese but, in retrospect, has certainly been a blessing both to India and to her friends.

Another aspect of Indian foreign policy which follows almost as a corollary to the policy of nonalignment is the policy of peaceful coexistence. The acceptance of the policy of peaceful coexistence comes naturally out of our own need to accommodate different religious views and cultures in India. We have tried throughout our history to bring about unity in diversity. It would be a dull world indeed if all were to think alike and all were to function alike. We want variety in this world, where people should be free to live their own lives and search for God in their own way. We should try to understand and to convince but not try to force our way of life on others.

World War II saw the end of European hegemony in Asia. Japanese conquest and brief occupation of Southeast Asia had ruined the prestige of the white man and had destroyed the very basis of colonial rule in the region. Even after Japan surrendered, the imperial powers were left so much weakened as a result of the war that they could no longer hope to hold on to their colonies. The two countries that emerged as the dominant powers in the postwar world are the United States and the Soviet Union. The wartime alliance between the two soon broke down and Washington and Moscow became the centers of two opposing ideologies. Anti-Communism became the basic policy of the United States and the Soviet Union claimed to be the champions against imperialism and colonialism. West Europeans who felt that their security was menaced by the Soviet Union joined the United States in the NATO alliance. East Europeans on the other hand joined the Soviet Union and became members of the Warsaw Pact to ensure their own security. Many other countries later joined one or the other alliance, with the result that the world was divided into two rival blocs.

India and many other newly emerging independent countries of Asia and Africa refused to join either bloc. In their view, these alliances do not promote peace. On the contrary, the division of the world into two hostile camps creates more suspicion and fear and threatens peace. In the nuclear age, a total war must be ruled out if the world is to be saved from complete destruction. The only alternative to tension, war and destruction is peaceful coexistence. For India, need for peace is not merely desirable but is vital. Faced with numerous problems at home which call for immediate attention, India requires a long period of peace, so that it may get time enough to solve these problems. India did not think there was any alternative to war other than a policy of peaceful coexistence. With a view to further this policy, India spared no efforts to lessen fear and suspicion, and assist in arriving at some mutual understanding even when no agreement was possible. India welcomed any development that brought the two superpowers together and also welcomed the decision of so many newly independent countries to follow a similar policy, since the adoption of that policy extended the area of peace. "Panch Sheel," or the Five Principles of Coexistence, were first formulated in the preamble to the agreement between India and China in regard to Tibet, which was signed on April 29, 1954. The immediate objective was to establish an area of peace on the Sino-Indian border, but these principles indicate the policy that India wanted to pursue in regard to these matters not only with China but also with all other countries. These principles are: (1) mutual respect for each other's territorial integrity and sovereignty; (2) mutual nonaggression; (3) mutual noninterference in each other's internal affairs; (4) sovereign equality and mutual benefit; and (5) peaceful coexistence. "Panch Sheel" was further elaborated into the "Ten Principles" adopted at the Bandung Conference held in 1955. By pledging to observe Panch Sheel, the countries concerned voluntarily agreed to restrain themselves from following certain courses of action. This is something like giving one his word of honor and, as such, it was believed that no country would find it easy to break this solemn pledge. It is true that a country can break this pledge, but then such a country would be bound no more by a formal treaty. One who is capable of breaking his word of honor and does not mind a moral condemnation is not likely to behave differently even if he is party to a binding treaty.

The United States also wants to cultivate friendly relations with all and is equally keen on peace. One has only to recall Lincoln's second inaugural address where he said, "With malice toward none; with charity for all; with firmness in the right, as God gives us to see the right, let us strive on to finish the work we are in." There is no difference whatsoever in the objectives of India and the U.S.A. but there is a considerable divergence of views on the means to achieve those objectives. To the Americans, there can be no doubt that the danger to peace comes only from the Communist countries or that this danger can only be met by the entire free world presenting a united front against it. In their view, it is immoral not to choose between right and wrong or to refuse to line up with the free world. Indians would point out in reply that they have indeed made their own choice. They have, after due consideration, chosen parliamentary democracy and they themselves prefer the democratic way of life. At the same time, they believe that every nation must be conceded the right to choose its own political philosophy and its own way of life. No country can claim all wisdom; nor has any country the right to force its way of life on others because it considers that to be the most desirable one. Indians do not think that it is any part of their duty to try to convert others to their way of life, with the zeal of a crusader. This is a feeling which has been ingrained in them by the Hindu religion which throughout its long history never encouraged proselytization. Some four thousand years ago, their scriptures taught them that "truth is one: men call it variously." Truth is not the monopoly of any race or any religion. Each country takes the path which it considers best suited to its needs. One may freely express his views but it is unwise to attempt to force those views on others. If some countries prefer totalitarianism, military dictatorship, basic democracy, guided democracy, parliamentary democracy or some other form of government, it is their business and should be no concern of outsiders so long as they do not try to force these systems on other countries. Many Americans, on the other hand, consider it to be their duty to try to convert other people to accept their standards, their ideas and aspirations. This is a basic difference between Indians and Americans. Free press, parliamentary democracy, free enterprise, are no doubt desirable—and Indians themselves have chosen them—but we realize that we have neither the right nor the power to impose our ideas of freedom on the world. We cannot make an unwilling people conform to our ideals and concepts, however desirable they may appear to us. We must recognize our limitations.

Indians also do not share the American belief that there are only two sides to each issue—black and white. In fact, there is no absolute black or absolute white. There are only infinite shades of gray in between—some darker than others. When an issue is clearly in the right or in the wrong, the choice is easy but the difficulty is that we often differ as to what is absolutely right and what is absolutely wrong. The development of McCarthyism showed what an atmosphere of fear and insecurity can be created by one man, even in democratic America, in the name of carrying on a crusade against Communism. The methods McCarthy used to acquire power are very similar to those used by Communists. There was little to choose between McCarthyism and Communism, since both destroyed individual freedom. Again, if leftist totalitarianism is bad, is rightist dictatorship very much better? Yet Portugal is an ally of the United States and is considered to be an important member of the free world! If one takes a close look, it would be clear that in a number of countries allied to the United States, there is not even a semblance of democracy. There is no freedom of thought, the press is controlled and sometimes there is not even the rule of law. Indians find it difficult to understand how the United States, the most powerful democracy in the world, can ally itself with reactionary dictatorial regimes, merely because the dictators claim to be anti-Communist. Some top American officials say that the United States will condone dictatorships provided on crucial matters of American interest their policies coincide with American wishes largely defined by anti-Communism. Progressive change is often looked upon with suspicion as being organized by Communists. It is not always appreciated that if peaceful changes become impossible, the entire underdeveloped world is almost bound to go in for violent revolutions. Socialism has a bad odor in America and the distinction between socialism and communism is often lost in the popular mind. American alliance with dictators does not always bring any political or economic benefit to the people over whom the dictators rule. Any attempt by the United States to liberalize the administration or to give some freedom to the people only antagonizes the dictator. In such regimes, economic aid seldom filters down to the masses. By including dictators in the "free world" the Americans have only debased the free world. The cause of democracy has certainly not been advanced by alliances with dictators. On the contrary, an impression has been created that individual freedom, freedom of the press, freedom of thought and the rule of law are of little consequence and that their absence can be condoned so long as the dictators are, or claim to be, anti-Communists.

In the Indian view, there is also apparently no great advantage in presenting a united front against Communism in military terms. So far as India and the rest of the underdeveloped world are concerned, Communism will have to be fought mainly on the economic front. The standard of living in India with a per capita income of $73 per annum is abnormally low. If we cannot improve the economic condition of the people, if we cannot give them better food and clothing, better housing, more employment, the risk of internal subversion cannot altogether be ruled out. Such military preparedness as an economically underdeveloped country can hope to achieve, would then be of little help. If the nuclear balance of terror does not prevent a world conflagration, the alliance with the United States of all the militarily weak countries will certainly be of no avail. A moral condemnation in the world forum by such countries may be much more useful than military support. If military support does ultimately become necessary, that may be forthcoming, but the nonaligned countries wish to retain the right to judge independently and determine for themselves the policy they should adopt.

Americans argue that in the ultimate analysis a superior

military might is the only effective check against a threat to peace. As Barry Goldwater put it, his was a message of "peace through preparedness." He said that "what we Americans need to understand is that a devotion to preparedness is a devotion to peace"! * Americans say that India's policy of nonalignment and of peaceful coexistence stems from its economic and industrial weakness. There is no doubt an element of truth in this analysis but there is nothing to be ashamed of. Every country, in formulating its foreign policy, must necessarily be guided by its own strength and its interests. India is fully conscious of its weaknesses. The difference in economic and industrial strength of India and the U.S.A. is certainly reflected in their respective foreign policies. Lacking economic and military strength, India has to follow a policy which the United States followed for close on a century and a half. The United States today is the strongest power in the world—both militarily and economically. It had no option but to assume the leadership of the Western world. It has tried to contain Communist expansion not only through diplomacy but by forming military alliances and by threats of retaliation. India, on the other hand, because of its past traditions, because of its weakness and because of the immensity of its own problems, had to pin its faith on mediation, conciliation and Panch Sheel. The United States believes that peace can be secured only through presenting a united front against Communism. India feels that the division of the world into two hostile camps only increases tension and may lead to war through accident or miscalculation.

After the massive Chinese attack on India in October 1962, many Americans have pointed out how wrong was the policy of India and how pathetic was the reliance of India on non-

* *The New York Times,* August 11, 1964.

alignment and Panch Sheel, which proved to be of no avail. It has also been urged that the belief that Communism will have to be fought mainly on the economic front has not been borne out by facts. In retrospect, one may no doubt with some justice blame India for not being realistic enough to prepare for the contingency of an attack from China. In fact, a considerable section of public opinion in India both in and outside Parliament blamed the Government of India for having neglected the defense of India ever since its independence. It is true that the Chinese have let us down. By accepting Panch Sheel and by subscribing to the Ten Principles adopted at the Bandung Conference, the Chinese lulled us into a false sense of security. They broke away from these commitments when it suited their purpose. One can perhaps take some consolation from the fact that an unscrupulous government could have similarly broken away from a more binding treaty. When Nehru was asked whether he would now agree that his policy of peaceful coexistence was wrong he replied that "our policy was completely correct. It is the policy of China which has not been correct." "It is true," he said, "that the ideals of Panch Sheel have been broken and are likely to be broken in future. The ideal of truth has often been broken and denied but that does not make truth untruth. A good ideal does not become a bad ideal if people do not act up to it. That may mean that the world was not yet ready for it." It is a curious coincidence that during negotiations with Japanese Ambassador Nomura in 1941, the U.S. Secretary of State, Mr. Cordell Hull, demanded an agreement on the following points:

(1) Respect for the territorial integrity and the sovereignty of each and all nations;

(2) support of the principle of noninterference in the internal affairs of other countries;

(3) support of the principle of equality, including equality of commercial opportunity;

(4) nondisturbance of the status quo in the Pacific except as the status quo may be altered by peaceful means.

The principles that the Japanese were asked to observe are virtually the same as those enshrined in Panch Sheel. It was no less unrealistic to expect the Japanese, then at the height of their power, to agree to observe these principles. In 1954–55 when China subscribed to Panch Sheel, the Chinese were certainly not as powerful. India can perhaps be forgiven for believing in the circumstances that the Chinese might restrain themselves from violating the principles which they had promised to observe. The difference, however, is that while the Japanese rejected these principles straightaway, the more wily Chinese accepted them and later broke their pledges. Before blaming India for not following a more realistic policy, one has to assume that India could have afforded to divert her meager resources toward defense without increasing the risk of internal subversion. We could not in any case have diverted enough of our resources to ensure an adequate defense against a massive Chinese attack without forgoing even the modest economic development that has been achieved. Few can be bold enough to assert that there would have been no risk of internal subversion in such a contingency. It is therefore difficult to say—even in retrospect—what the realistic policy of India should have been. In fact, there is a consensus today that one of the objectives of the Chinese in attacking India was to force India to divert adequate resources to its defense, thereby slowing down the pace of economic development.

Our sad experience with China has no doubt proved that in our efforts to concentrate all our resources toward achieving a more rapid economic development, we had gone to the other extreme and had taken too great a risk by not providing for adequate defense. Incidentally, however, our experience has proved that the division of the world into two groups, Communist and non-Communist, has now really little meaning. The Soviet Union, for example, to the great annoyance of the Chinese, maintained its neutrality in the Sino-Indian conflict and later gave India both moral and some material support. It was one of the principal grievances of the Chinese against the Soviet Union that it supported a nonaligned country, in preference to a sister socialist country.

Indians do not therefore accept the proposition that there is no difference between one Communist country and another. On the contrary, they believe that there is a great deal of difference between the Soviet Union and Communist China. Moscow realizes the dangers of a nuclear war while Peking believes, or says it believes, in the inevitability of war and thinks that out of the ashes of destruction will emerge a much better world of the future. Moscow believes in peaceful coexistence. The Soviet leaders think that they will in any case win the race of economic development and once their methods are proved to be superior, other countries will automatically adopt them. There is, therefore, no need to take the risk of destroying, through another war, all that it has built up at tremendous cost during the last half century. Peking, on the other hand, has little to lose and believes that there may even be something to gain. This basic difference in outlook is mainly due to the relative economic development of the two countries. Peking will also perhaps be less militant when it has succeeded in building up its economy to a higher level. This development may take a couple of decades. There are some people in the United States who recognize this difference and consider China as posing the greatest threat to the free world. Others think that there is no force in the argument that "fat Communists are less dangerous than the lean ones." In their view China, being poorer and weaker, is far less of a menace than the Soviet Union and will continue to be so at least for the next quarter of a century. Because of our geographical proximity to China and because of our recent experience, we believe China to be a much greater threat than the Soviet Union from whom we have so far received nothing but sympathy and support.

The thawing in the Cold War is already noticeable and the blocs are showing signs of breaking up. The relaxation of tension has reduced fear and suspicion. The small and medium powers now feel somewhat reassured of their security and no longer see any desperate need to continue as loyal members of a bloc. The Sino-Soviet differences have come out in the open. The monolithic structure of the powerful Soviet bloc has started to crack. China appears on the world scene as an aggressive expansionist power with an intensely nationalistic outlook. Many of the smaller countries in the socialist bloc are now showing a great deal of independent thinking. France has virtually withdrawn from SEATO and her progressive withdrawal from NATO would no doubt weaken the Western alliance. President de Gaulle is reported to have said at a news conference held on July 23, 1964,* "For the countries of the free world, above all for those menaced by the ambitions of the Soviets, it was almost inevitable that they accept American leadership. The new world was, among them all, the greatest victor. The Atlantic Alliance under the command of the United States which was armed with atomic bombs, guaranteed their security. . . . Things have obviously changed because the Western countries of our ancient conti-

* *The New York Times* of July 24, 1964.

nent have rebuilt their economy and are in the process of rebuilding their military strength. . . . The Soviet empire is seeing China contest its domination of vast areas of Asia and sees European satellites edging away, by however little that may be." President de Gaulle concluded by saying, "Given all this, the result is that the partition of the world into two camps respectively led by Washington and Moscow no longer corresponds to the new situation." The NATO allies—Greece and Turkey—were almost on the verge of war over Cyprus. As *The New York Times* said in an editorial on August 9, 1964: "This latest exacerbation of hostility brought Greece and Turkey to the brink of a conflict that would be ruinous for them, for Cyprus and for the Western alliance. The tragedy implicit in all this is specially keen for Americans because, if war does come, both sides will wage it with weapons provided them by the United States—weapons supplied to strengthen defense against possible Communist aggression and not for senseless fratricidal conflict among fellow members of NATO." Communist China and North Vietnam know that Pakistan, despite its membership in SEATO, is aloof and has withheld support for the United States in its actions in Vietnam. The Philippines and Thailand are both somewhat disenchanted with SEATO. SEATO and NATO are thus already somewhat split.

At the same time, signs are not wanting to indicate that the two superpowers are perceptibly, if slowly, coming together. Both sides are looking for ways and means of further relaxing the existing tensions. Following nuclear confrontation over Cuba, there has been a progressive realization on both sides that since a total war has become impossible in a nuclear age, total victory is equally unattainable. A war between the two would mean only destruction for both. A compromise has thus now become inevitable. If an agreed compromise formula cannot be found, the parties must agree to differ and leave it at that and neither party should attempt to impose its own will on the other by force. There is now considerable doubt in the U.S.A. about the efficacy, in present-day conditions, of trying military solutions to problems which are basically of a political or economic nature. All this development arises out of a recognition of the fact that there is no alternative to peaceful coexistence. Another significant development is the desire—now evident—of the two superpowers to come to agreement through direct negotiations. The Moscow Treaty on a nuclear test ban, as also the setting up of the "hot line," were the results of such direct negotiation. So were the agreements not to place the nuclear weapons in outer space and on the principles regarding the formulation of a space code. Greater cooperation in carrying on activities in outer space is now being seriously advocated as both countries realize the desirability of avoiding wasteful expenditure on space programs. Sooner rather than later there is bound to be a further rapprochement between the two superpowers. When that comes, rival blocs will have to disappear. There would then be no blocs left to align with. Nonalignment and peaceful coexistence would then become the order of the day. Strangely enough, the very cooperation between the two superpowers, their desire to lessen tensions and their anxiety to avoid confrontation have caused some dissatisfaction among some of the small powers. This dissatisfaction found expression in the statements of some delegations in the 19th Session of the General Assembly. Mr. Guevara of Cuba said, "Imperialism, particularly U.S. imperialism, has attempted to have the world believe that peaceful coexistence is the exclusive right of the great powers. . . . At present the type of peaceful coexistence to which we aspire, does not exist in

many cases." * Mr. Subandrio of Indonesia said, "The growing degree of peaceful coexistence between the capitalist
lands and the Communist world—which is commendable indeed—regrettably has not brought with it, peaceful coexistence for the new developing countries." ** Mr. Coulibaly of
Mali also said, "The small powers and the developing countries labored under the illusion that there was a relaxation of
tension between the East and the West, and they worked to
codify the principles of peaceful coexistence, but while they
did so imperialism openly interfered in the internal affairs
of the young states and prevented the implementation of international agreements which are not consonant with their
sordid interests." † The Chinese and their followers of course
do not have any faith in peaceful coexistence. One cannot
therefore confidently predict that there will be no blocs in
the future under new leadership.

Many Americans themselves are conscious of the need for
American foreign policy to adapt itself to changing circumstances. In an illuminating address in the American Senate
on March 25, 1964, Senator J. W. Fulbright, Chairman of the
Senate Foreign Relations Committee, spoke on "Old Myths
and New Realities" of American foreign policy. In this
thought-provoking address Senator Fulbright said that the
character of the Cold War has, for the present at least, been
profoundly altered and he called for a more realistic foreign
policy. In his view, peaceful coexistence has in the changed
circumstances become part of the present-day American foreign policy. The views expressed by him are, however, not
yet shared by many others, who challenge some of the basic
assumptions of the Senator. Against the Senator's view that

---

* 1299th Plenary meeting, December 11, 1964.
** 1300th Plenary meeting, December 11, 1964.
† 1319th Plenary Meeting, January 21, 1965.

the Soviet Union has withdrawn from "extremely aggressive policies," it is argued that the Soviet Union had no occasion to pursue such aggressive policies when it could achieve its objectives by a mere threat of war. Unlike Senator Fulbright, they still believe in the policy of brinkmanship. It is their complaint that due to an exaggerated fear of a nuclear war, the American Administration no longer goes in for a bold policy. It follows, instead, a policy of appeasement, with the result that the Soviet Union gets away with its demands. Curiously enough, that is precisely Peking's criticism of the Soviet policy—that the Soviet Union is unnecessarily worried about the American "paper tiger" and is always capitulating to the imperialists. Thus the extreme right and the extreme left meet. Both want to play the game of bluff without realizing that the stakes are far too high. While each expects to stop at the brink, neither seems to realize that the slightest miscalculation may make it too late to avoid falling into the abyss. Adlai Stevenson is reported to have coupled Senator Barry Goldwater's position on world affairs with that of Chinese Communists. He said, "The two ends of the political spectrum, like the two ends of the turning fork, often vibrate in harmony. Both extremes in international politics are lethal and for the same reason—they ignore the fragility of man's survival; they play deadly games on the brink of disaster; they misread the facts of power and the restraints of responsibility; they gamble with the very precondition of our survival in the nuclear age." * It may be recalled that Senator Goldwater had opposed the ratification of the test ban treaty just as Peking is opposed to it. An article in *Izvestia* quoted Mr. Mao Tse-tung as having said five years ago, "We learned a lot from John Foster Dulles. He is our teacher. His policy

* *The New York Times*, August 14, 1964.

of brinkmanship was directed against us but we learned it and used it over the island of Quemoy." * Mr. Mao could equally claim that his views on nonalignment coincided with those of Mr. Dulles. According to the Chinese Communists there can be no policy of nonalignment which is at best a state of unstable equilibrium to be replaced naturally by a more stable alliance with one bloc or the other. Mr. Mao had no "illusions about a third road."

Leaving out of consideration the views on the extreme right and the extreme left, it is probably correct to say that there is today much less criticism of the policy of nonalignment and peaceful coexistence. There is a greater realization of the fact that there is no satisfactory alternative to peaceful coexistence. In any case, the way rival blocs are cracking up, it seems that most countries will soon have to be nonaligned. In these circumstances, it is not unreasonable to expect that these basic aspects of Indian foreign policy will now at least be better understood, even if one cannot entirely agree with them. In retrospect, one may rightly point out the failure of the Indian policy of peaceful coexistence since it could not prevent the Chinese Communists' attack on India, but that does not necessarily mean that the policy itself was wrong. At any rate, our faith in our basic policy of peaceful coexistence has not been completed shattered. The Chinese rejection of Panch Sheel has, however, forced on the government and the public opinion a process of rethinking. There is a greater recognition of the need to adapt our policy to the changing circumstances. The policy of peaceful coexistence with others will still continue, but so far as our relation with China is concerned, we must be realists and build up our defense at least to that extent as would convince the Chinese that aggres-

* Reproduced in *The New York Times*, June 19, 1964.

sion will not pay. The Chinese aggression brought along with it the realization that a balance of nuclear terror may prevent total wars but it cannot prevent local wars even though they may have serious regional consequences. Events also belied the hope that military alliance with the West would stand in the way of Pakistan's building up close ties with Peking. A criticism that we should have had this knowledge from the beginning may now seem to be justified, but then one cannot always expect to be gifted with hindsight. Aggressors can count on the element of surprise and have an initial advantage. An economically weak country cannot permanently remain prepared for such attacks.

If the Indian policy is to be condemned for this reason, one could with equal justice say, in retrospect, that the American policy of containment of Communism through alliances was unnecessary to begin with and has now been proved to be a failure. This would not, however, be a fair criticism. In the immediate postwar years the fear of Soviet expansion may have justified the creation of NATO, and this alliance may have helped in the maintenance of peace in Europe. Again, mutual fear could justify the Warsaw Pact even though NATO always proclaimed itself to be a defensive alliance. As the risk of war receded, fear which brought the smaller and medium powers into these alliances also disappeared. They became less interested in the alliances and became more vocal in asserting their independence of the leaders of the blocs. The utility of continuing alliances today is therefore open to doubt. On the other hand, the creation of SEATO, in 1954, was from the very beginning a futile attempt at containment of Communism. There was little advantage in bringing together some weak states and giving them military aid when they were desperately in need of economic development and social reform. It would certainly not be profitable to pursue this line of criticism. It would be much more correct to say that the American and Indian foreign policies were perhaps both appropriate for the countries concerned in the circumstances in which they were placed at the time. It would be wrong however to cling to policies which may have now lost their utility. We must always be prepared to adapt our policies to changing circumstances. Indians must learn the lessons of the Chinese aggression and wake up to reality. Americans must realize that if they fight a war in Vietnam, they may have to fight alone without their SEATO allies.

COLONIALISM AND RACIALISM

THE bitter hostility of Indians to colonialism is not quite understood in America and many Americans consider this attitude somewhat unreasonable. Americans point out that they themselves have had a colonial past and while they recognize colonialism as an evil, they cannot understand why it should continue to arouse such bitter memories. They resent the fact that they are not given full credit for their anticolonial record and they wonder why their anticolonialism should sometimes appear to be suspect in Afro-Asian eyes. The difference in the attitudes of India and the U.S.A. toward colonialism is mainly due to their historical background. There is a fundamental difference in the nature of colonialism as experienced by Americans and that experienced by Indians. The British colonies in the North American continent, Australia or New Zealand must be distinguished from British possessions in Asia and Africa. They were loosely designated as colonies when, in fact, they should have been more appropriately described as "dependencies," as indeed India was so described before its independence. The colonists who settled down in North America were mainly of the same British stock, and they had the same historical and cultural background as the people in Britain. They had practically all the rights and privileges of a Britisher at home and they could always return home if they did not like the colonies. They had no reason to feel ashamed of being counted as British subjects and as Britishers they had no difficulty in owing their loyalty to the Crown. Some colonists continued to be loyal even during the American War of Independence and quite a few United Empire Loyalists migrated to Canada, rather than remain as citizens of a republican U.S.A. It is true that the colonists did not have the right to vote, but then very few people had this right even in England, in those days. It is also true that there was a certain amount of economic exploitation by the mother country but it was bearable and on the whole the colonies still continued to prosper. Admittedly, the aim of the British colonial system was to secure some ultimate benefit for Britain. Administration of colonies had therefore to be regulated so as to further the well-being of the mother country both economically and politically. Even so, an effective democracy in the colonies stood in the way of full enforcement of this British colonial policy. The British wanted to impose taxes on the colonists and raise revenues to be administered by the British Parliament. Whether the British measures were tyrannical or not, the fact remains that they appeared to be so to the colonists and that is what mattered. They opposed taxation without adequate representation. The Americans thus fought not against a foreign rule but against arbitrary government from London, which was no doubt often irritating to them. They opposed a colonial system which they considered to be against their economic interests. There were of course other factors leading to the War of Independence but there was certainly no feeling that an alien rule had been imposed on the colonists against their will.

The position was entirely different in the case of India and, for the matter of that, other European dependencies in Asia and Africa. In our case, there was of course economic exploitation, only to a much greater degree. Many of our thriving industries were deliberately destroyed and India was ruled at least for the first hundred years or so mainly with the object of securing the best interests of Great Britain. What was even more important is that not only was a foreign rule imposed upon us—peoples of different race, religion and color—but it brought in its wake racialism with attendant contempt for the Indian and intolerance of his way of life. We had a proud history of our own but we were subjected to humiliation and degradation by reason of the pigment of our skin. Political domination brought in its train the doctrine of racial superiority and arrogance among the governing classes. Colonialism in our case thus came to be closely associated with racialism. That is why it arouses a bitterness and a passion which Americans cannot even imagine. It is because we suffered so much from this aspect of colonial rule in the past that we are so uncompromisingly against colonialism and racialism in any form. To the Americans, colonialism is bad but they cannot understand why it deserves so much condemnation or why so much passion should be roused. To us colonialism, which is inextricably associated with racialism, is an unmitigated evil with which no compromise is possible. It is because of our respective history and experience that we are differently conditioned toward colonialism. That is why we have not always been able to see eye to eye with Americans on some colonial issues.

Racialism has been and continues to be the worst feature of colonial rule. The word native lost its etymological meaning and when spelt with a capital N came to mean a member of a non-European primitive and uncivilized race. The fact that everybody other than one of European descent was designated as a "Native," and as such was considered as primitive or uncivilized, hurt even more than the fact of colonial domination. With the honorable exception of eminent European scholars who made a special study of Asian culture and civilization, the average European showed nothing but contempt for everything Oriental. He did not know much of our proud and eventful past or of the important role played by Asians in world history or of the liberal contribution made by Asia to the civilization and culture of the world. Chinese, Hindu and Arab contributions to science, arts and philosophy still evoke admiration. It is from Central Asia that the Indo-Aryan people were believed to have spread all over the vast Eurasian continents. It is Asia that gave the world all its major religions —Hinduism, Buddhism, Confucianism, Judaism, Christianity and Islam. The earliest traces of civilization were found in different parts of Asia. Mighty empires with advanced civilizations were to be found in different parts of Asia, long before the Europeans came. Trade in luxury goods flowed from Asia to Europe over land and sea. Then came a period of stagnation, when Asia lost its drive and initiative and became completely moribund. Weakened by internal rivalries, Asia fell an easy prey to the more dynamic and adventurous Europeans. Europe then took the lead and forged ahead in science and technology. The center of the world, as it were, moved to Europe from where flowed all the streams of culture, arts and science. During the last couple of centuries, Europe virtually ruled the world and the history of Europe became practically the history of the world.

During the colonial era the European rulers played down the high level of civilization that had been achieved in Asia. Europeans gave the impression that they ruled in Asia not by reason of their superior knowledge of science and technology but because they represented a superior race. Political domination thus brought along with it contempt and humiliation for peoples with proud history and ancient civilization. The principle of white superiority pervaded the entire field of political, economic and social life in the colonial territories. Europeans lived away from the indigenous people and few cared to study the language or the civilization of the people. They not only took over political control but also controlled the entire colonial economy. In fact, they constituted a privileged class. Even when there was no actual colonial rule, as in West Asia and China, the doctrine of racial superiority was asserted and strictly enforced. The British and the Czarist Russian spheres of influence in Iran and the extraterritorial jurisdiction of certain European powers in China gave them not only opportunities of economic exploitation but also permitted social exclusiveness and other special privileges for the European.

Toward the latter part of the nineteenth century, nationalist movements of various types developed in different colonial territories. All these movements had three common characteristics—an assertion of racial equality, a demand for complete political power and a desire for full economic development. The demand for independence is thus closely related to the assertion of racial equality. They are really two separate aspects of the same nationalist movement. One objective could not be achieved without achieving the other. For over a century, Europeans had ruled their colonies on the theory of white superiority—a theory which the colonial people had willy-nilly accepted. Japan's successful attempt to shake off this inferiority and later her victory at the beginning of this century over Imperial Russia sent a thrill of admiration throughout Asia. For the first time after a century, the Asian began to question the validity of the theory of white superiority. It became increasingly intolerable to admit that the European was, because of his color, superior to the Asian. Much of the extreme bitterness that existed in the colonies— a bitterness which happily is almost past history now—can be attributed to racial arrogance of the European rulers. The superiority complex had gone so far that an Englishman whose pronunciation of English was worse than that of a London cockney could and did get away with refusing to travel in the same railway compartment with an Indian educated at Oxford or Cambridge. The white man could always demand a superior position vis-à-vis the black man irrespective of his education or his wealth.

It took a long time in India to put an end to this state of affairs. Alienation of the local intelligentsia brought up in an atmosphere of European thought and ideals has been one of the principal causes of the rise of Indian nationalism or, for the matter of that, nationalist movements in most colonial countries. The leaders of such nationalist movements were often people educated in Europe or America. They were surprised to find the European at home kind, courteous and considerate. They were often champions of fair deals and exponents of high moral principles. An Indian in England had all the rights and privileges of a British subject. True, there was occasionally an unpleasant experience of color prejudice but by and large there was hardly any discrimination between him and other British subjects of European origin. He found it difficult to understand how the European "east of the Suez" could develop a different code of conduct, give up his high moral principles and come to believe in racial superiority and in his divine mission to civilize the unwilling Asian or African. The lofty principles of liberty, equality and fraternity enunciated during the French Revolution were apparently intended only for the benefit of Frenchmen in France and not for the subject people outside its borders. It is indeed somewhat remarkable that most of the French empire, denying liberty, equality and fraternity to the inhabitants thereof, was acquired after the French Revolution.

Today, we hear of the likelihood of a West European political union emerging soon out of the already achieved economic union. The concept of European solidarity as against the "Native" had, however, grown up in the East long ago. While Europeans were constantly fighting among themselves not only in Europe but over their colonies, in Asia and Africa, they did show a great deal of community of interest in their treatment of the local people. It was not the Englishman who ruled India or the Dutchman who ruled Indonesia or the Frenchman who ruled Indochina, but it was the European who ruled over these territories. A European alien, even an erstwhile enemy, had more social rights and privileges in India than a British subject of Indian descent. It was this concept of European unity vis-à-vis Asians, this concept of racial superiority, that was responsible for such Asian solidarity as has been developed now—a development born out of a common antagonism toward the Europeans, based on their treatment of Asians. In no country in Asia was there much of an Asian feeling as such but the European practice of grouping them together as Asians gave rise to the concept of an

"Asian" which gradually came to be accepted in Asia as well. Today there is undoubtedly the beginning of a feeling of some solidarity among Asians. The newly emerging African states have had similar experience of racialism and colonialism. It is therefore natural that there should now be a community of interest between Asians and Africans. Before independence, there was very little contact between the peoples of African and Asian colonies. On attaining independence, these erstwhile colonies could, however, get in touch with one another. The people of Asia and Africa have bitter memories of racialism, political domination and of economic exploitation. No wonder therefore that these are the main planks on which Asia and Africa are united. It is against this background that one should try to understand Afro-Asian solidarity on questions of racialism and colonialism.

For India—and for Afro-Asians in general—racialism is thus inextricably linked up with colonialism. That is why our views on colonialism sometimes appear to be extreme to Americans whose colonial past was free from any experience of racialism. India has always fought against colonialism and racialism in any form. The attitude of the United States on colonialism and racialism has not always been consistent. There was a time right up to and during World War II when the traditional anticolonialism of the United States irritated European colonial powers. Winston Churchill's annoyance with Roosevelt for his support for self-government in India is well known.

Even after the war, the United States of America gave wholehearted support to Indonesia in its struggle for freedom, much to the annoyance of the Dutch. With the advent of the Cold War, the American attitude toward colonial struggles, however, became somewhat cautious because it was considered inexpedient to rub the colonial powers too much the wrong way, particularly as they all happened to be allies. Americans also found some of the colonies useful from their own point of view as military bases, or potential ones. They had therefore to make some compromises with their anticolonial tradition, and this did not escape notice. The French were assisted with money and materials in the hope that they would be able to hold on to their colonies in Indochina. That hope did not materialize. It is unkind of President de Gaulle now to imply that U.S. interests in Indochina are colonialist. At a news conference held on July 23, 1964,* he was reported to have said: "The Americans at the time assumed everywhere in the world ... the burden of defense against Communism. Since South Vietnam was obviously exposed to it ... the Americans decided to put South Vietnam in a condition to defend itself. I believe one can add, without hurting our American friends, that their conviction that they were fulfilling a sort of vocation and also their aversion to all colonial activity, which was not theirs, and finally the very natural desire in such a powerful people to take up new positions, all this determined them to take over Indochina from France." It did however hurt and Americans naturally resented the suggestion that the United States had taken over Indochina from France, when in fact it had given all possible assistance to France to hold on to these colonies.

On racialism again, the U.S. attitude was somewhat ambivalent. Americans, while expressing their abhorrence of apartheid, were reluctant to join condemnatory resolutions in the UN, in the first few years, on the ground that this was entirely a matter of domestic jurisdiction for South Africa. As African

* *The New York Times,* dated July 24, 1964.

pressure mounted with increased African membership of the UN, the United States found it necessary to change its policy and support anti-apartheid resolutions. Americans believe that Indians are too much exercised about colonialism, which in any case is dying out, but are too little concerned with the dangers of Communism. Indians on the other hand—and also most Afro-Asians—think that Americans emphasize lack of freedom in Communist countries but do little or nothing about the denial of elementary human rights to the Africans in South Africa, Angola or Mozambique.

Americans may well be right up to a point when they say that colonialism is not such an unmitigated evil as Afro-Asians imagine. They point out, with some justice, that colonialism brought about law and order as well as security of life and property; in many cases it opened up and developed countries which were backward. The people did not know what was best for them and it was the colonial administrator with a missionary zeal who knew and did what was good for them. There may be an element of truth in all this but the fact remains that colonialism asserted white supremacy and denied the right to people to govern themselves. This was intolerable. The inhabitants of colonies were, in Kipling's words, "lesser breeds" who were naturally expected to submit to the white man who was always to be in a privileged position. Colonial rulers seldom understood the people or their hopes and aspirations. While the colonial administration maintained law and order, it rarely did anything to improve social and economic conditions and was almost invariably opposed to any industrialization which, it was feared, might disturb the pattern of trade between the colonies and the metropolitan country concerned. This was a shortsighted policy, for it not only prevented a further utilization of the natural resources of the colonies but also stood in the way of their acquiring any technical know-how and taking an appropriate place in the world of today. All economic and social development was frozen, as it were, with the result that most colonies faced serious problems on their independence and have had to start from scratch. As to the benefits of law and order, John Strachey had this to say with reference to the early stages of British rule in India: "By the late eighteenth century, Bengal which Orme begins his history by describing as 'a paradise' had been reduced in spite of . . . or because of, her conquerors having suppressed civil conflict and introduced their form of 'law and order,' to the most pitiable conditions. Large tracts of its countryside had been depopulated and had reverted to jungle, its cities were in decay, its people starving." * The fringe benefits of a colonial regime are nothing compared to its much more serious failings which have hampered the growth and development of the colonial people. If the colonial issue has been dealt with at some length, it is not with the object of criticizing that system but with a view to enable one to understand the background against which the Indian attitude on colonialism and racialism has to be judged.

It is often argued that India attacks only Western colonialism, but does not show any such opposition to Soviet colonialism. Apparently, in the American view, there are three different types of Soviet colonialism, spread over Europe and Asia. In the first category are placed the East European countries which are described as Soviet satellites, where Soviet troops are stationed. It is, however, difficult to accept the proposition that these countries are in any way colonies or dependencies. If they were not independent sovereign states, how could they become members of the UN? The West should not

* John Strachey, *The End of Empire*, page 44.

have agreed to admit them—many as founder members of the UN. It is true that Soviet troops have been or are still stationed in some of these countries. India has always been in favor of withdrawal of foreign troops from all countries but it also recognizes the sovereign right of every state to enter into defensive agreements with other states permitting the stationing in their territories of the troops of such allies. Presence of foreign troops with the consent of the states concerned does not mean that they are colonies. If the Soviet Union has maintained troops in the territories of their allies of the Warsaw Pact, so have Americans maintained troops, or retained bases, in the territories of many of their allies.

In the second category of Soviet colonies are included Latvia, Lithuania and Estonia. It is argued that the Soviet Union has recently incorporated these countries into its own territory. It is apparently forgotten that these three countries had long been part of European Russia and were separated as independent states only after World War I. Their separate existence might never have come about but for the Bolshevik Revolution. In any case, against independence for less than a quarter of a century must be taken into account the fact that in the period prior to World War I they were integral parts of Czarist Russia. With this historical background, it is as difficult for us to treat them as colonies, as it would be to treat Scotland or Wales as colonies of England or to consider Burgundy as a colony of France. We would then have to question the legality of Germany or of Italy which grew into single states after nationally integrating a number of independent principalities. There may be an element of truth in the Western criticism that Africans and Asians are exercised over colonialism only when it means white rule over black, brown or yellow people. As has been stated before, in the eyes of African and Asians the worst feature of colonialism is racialism, which was always associated with it. When there is no racial prejudice, it is not easy for them to identify colonialism unless the ethnic difference between the peoples concerned is clearly noticeable. We really do not know to what extent the people of Latvia, Lithuania or Estonia are racially different from the people of contiguous territories in the Soviet Union. We have no knowledge that the Russians practice any racial discrimination against them. If they are treated alike, that takes away much of the sting of colonialism. The Irish had been demanding independence and the Scots had been sporadically asking for home rule, but so far as India was concerned, they were all British and they all had the same rights and privileges in India as against Indians. Until the Irish actually started fighting against the English, we in India saw little difference between them. They all belonged to the ruling race and had the same attitude toward India. There was a quip current in India to the effect that "the Irishman fought and the Englishman won India for the benefit of the Scot." The reference was to the fact that the Irish produced some of the best generals in the British Indian Army and that big business was mostly in the hands of the Scots—and still is, at least in the city of Calcutta. The ethnic difference between the ruler and the ruled had been given importance not only by Africans and Asians but also by Europeans. The Turkish and the Arab rules—the only non-European rules—of Europe were much more hated than rule by European emperors. One has only to recall the passionate outbursts by liberal Englishmen over alleged Turkish atrocities on Greeks, outbursts which are comparable to the vehemence of present-day condemnation of Portuguese rule or misrule of Angola and Mozambique.

In the last category of Soviet colonies are mentioned the Asian Republics of the Soviet Union. People in these republics are no doubt ethnically different from those of European Russia. Russian expansion over the land mass of Asia—and beyond, as far as Alaska—in the Czarist days was certainly a classic example of imperialism. It was, however, at the same time an expansion into an adjoining vast open space—filling up a vacuum as it were. This is in some ways comparable to what happened in North and South America. The European colonists drove away the aborigines and spread themselves out all over the American continents. In fact, the American Indian population was virtually exterminated in North America, although substantial numbers still remain in Latin America. Those that have survived are not treated as people under colonial rule. The nomadic tribes in Asian territories of Russia, however, somehow managed to survive the Czarist rule. Curiously enough, no nationalist movements demanding independence grew up, as they did in almost all the colonies of the West European powers. Czarist rule was oppressive, but then it was no less oppressive even in European Russia. The worker or the peasant shared the misery that was the common lot of everyone whether in European or Asian Russia. The treatment of different peoples varied only according to their status in the hierarchy. There was not so much difference in treatment as existed between people in the colonies and those in the metropolitan countries of West Europe. The revolt against the Czarist rule therefore came as a class struggle and did not have racial overtones. Even after the Bolshevik revolution, there was not much difference in the lot of the common man, no matter what his ethnic origin was. In the Stalin era, the people, whether in the European or in the Asian territories, were all subjected to the same hardships and privations. When economic and social improvement came, this was shared more or less equally by people all over the country. There was no obvious discrimination in this respect and racial prejudice, if there was any, was not so apparent and was certainly not practiced so offensively as it was in colonies of other European powers. The grant by the Soviet central authority of full autonomy in these Asian republics and the efforts to develop them into modern societies in much the same way as in European Russia apparently prevented the growth of a separate nationalism. The Asian republics have the same type of representation in the central government as have European republics. In many ways their position is similar to Hawaii, which is a constituent state of the U.S.A., even though its inhabitants are of different ethnic groups.

Industrial development in Asian republics was not only not opposed as was almost invariably the case in the colonies of West Europe, but after the revolution, was even encouraged. A number of important factories were in fact set up in remote areas—maybe for greater military security but nevertheless to the economic benefit of the local people. One of the strongest criticisms against colonial rule used to be the neglect of education of the indigenous people. Asian republics of the Soviet Union present a glaring contrast. The educational advance, specially in science and technology, has been spectacular and literacy has gone up by leaps and bounds. The highest priority was accorded to education and the nomads were persuaded to accept a settled life either in agriculture or in industry. The Asian republics were opened up through a system of transport and communication, in much the same way as European Russia. Absence of discriminatory treatment and of racial prejudice helped in the process of integration and reconciliation. The essential prerequisites for the growth of nationalist movements demanding racial equality as well as political and economic freedom were therefore wanting. We in India have had firsthand knowledge of Western colonialism. We also knew of strong national movements in other colonial territories, which we supported. Until recently we knew little of the Soviet Union and had no knowledge of any freedom movement in any part of the Soviet Union. The question of supporting such movements did not therefore arise. If and when conditions in the Asian republics of the Soviet Union change and nationalist movements develop, demanding secession and independence, there will be time enough then for other countries to consider raising their voice in support. So long as there is no such demand from the Asian republics, outsiders cannot and should not promote or develop separatist tendencies. If there had been no racial discrimination and if serious efforts had been made to make the colonial people feel that they were on a footing of complete equality with people in the metropolitan area, nationalist movements might not have developed in so many colonies of West European powers. In the absence of such powerful movements among the people themselves, outsiders could not possibly have initiated or promoted a demand for independence.

Racial prejudice and a superiority complex have not been the monopoly of the white people. Most other people have been guilty of these failings in varying degrees. These failings on the part of non-Europeans, however, did not very much matter since they did not have the power to enforce acceptance of their alleged superiority—at any rate, over a large area. Such prejudice shown by Europeans, at a time when they controlled virtually the whole of Asia and Africa, has done incalculable damage. The growth of some kind of solidarity among Afro-Asians as a reaction against European practice of racial discrimination has a dangerous potentiality unless the principles of racial equality is genuinely accepted and sincerely implemented without any further delay. We should not be oblivious to the attempts that are already being made to exploit racial feelings to build up an anti-Western front. It is bad enough to have rival ideological blocs. It would be much worse if the world were to be divided into two or more racial blocs in the future.

INDIAN ECONOMIC POLICY

COLONIALISM AND RACIALISM | 81

T HE foreign policy of a country is naturally closely linked with its economic policy. There is still some misconception in the United States about the Indian economic policy. Our declared objective of achieving the goal of a socialistic pattern of society has been very much misunderstood. This objective is in conformity with the provisions in our Constitution which require the state to secure a social order in which justice, social, economic and political, shall prevail. Broadly speaking, what we mean to develop is a society in which there is social cohesion, a society which is classless and casteless and in which there is equality of opportunity for all and the possibility for everyone to live a full life. Obviously this goal can not be attained unless we can produce more wealth for distribution. When we lay stress on the need for the removal of disparities, we do not intend to reach that goal by expropriating the few rich and spread out poverty. We desire to develop an economic system which "does not result in the concentration of wealth and means of production to the common detriment." Whether one calls these principles socialistic or not, they have undoubtedly been the objectives in all Western democracies over a long period. Equality of opportunity and social justice, which are our objectives, have reached a much higher level in the U.S.A. today than we can hope to achieve in many years to come.

Socialism is something which is anathema to the average American. It conjures up all kinds of images, loss of freedom and individuality, and killing of free enterprise. To the American, socialism and communism are apparently synonymous. Many Communists call themselves Socialists, as indeed many Communist countries call themselves "People's Democracies." We are trying to bring about a socialistic pattern of society but there is no country which has greater freedom and individuality than one finds in India. In fact, in India individualism not only prevents regimentation but sometimes goes to the other extreme and stands in the way of organized, collective or cooperative action. True, there is governmental control in certain sectors of Indian industry but even so the public sector in Indian economy today is proportionately much smaller than that in the U.S.A. While we are still talking of a socialistic pattern of society, this has already been achieved to a far greater extent in the U.S.A. Free enterprise is still responsible for almost 90 percent of India's national output while the comparable figure for the U.S.A. is about 80 percent. American suspicion of our economic policy is thus largely misplaced. The Indian policy does not venture to go as far as the policies followed by the Labour government in the United Kingdom. All that we want is that the state should step in only in those fields of production in which private capital is shy either because of the risk involved or because of the lack of adequate or immediate return.

For a proper appreciation of our economic policy it is necessary to have some knowledge of the shattered economy we inherited on our independence. During the long period of colonial rule our economy had been practically stagnant and had failed to meet the demands of a rapidly growing population or to relieve the pressure on agriculture—about 70 percent of the working population is engaged in agriculture. Agricultural yields were, however, low in comparison with those in most other countries. Large-scale industries provided employment for about only 10 percent of the working population; medium and small-scale industries engaged another 10 percent and the remaining 10 percent found employment in services and in the distributive trade. Scarcity of the barest essentials of life, relatively high prices and a low level of consumption underlined the inadequacy of the country's economy.

On top of these long-term trends which explain the persistence of mass poverty, an extraordinarily severe strain was put on the Indian economy by World War II and by the partition of the country. Under the stimulus of war demands, some increase in agricultural and industrial production did take place. But as India became the supply base for the allied armies east of Suez, this increase in production was more than offset by the diversion to war purposes of a large proportion of the total supplies available. The value of goods and services provided by the economy of undivided India for war purposes was roughly equivalent to four and a half billion dollars. The diversion of the limited resources of such a poor people inevitably led to undernourishment, poor health and a consequent reduction in productive capacity culminating in the death by starvation of a couple of million people during the Bengal famine in 1943. A further severe shock was received when the country was partitioned, on our independence. Partition resulted in certain fundamental changes in the economic structure of the country. A part of what had previously been internal trade in cotton, jute and food grains now became a feature of external trade, resulting in an aggravation of the balance of payments problem. While 82 percent of the population of the Indo-Pakistan subcontinent remained in India after partition, only 69 percent of the irrigated area, 65 percent of the wheat- and 68 percent of the rice-growing area fell to India's share. In consequence, food shortage was more aggravated. The jute mills remained in India, but the area growing jute went mostly to Pakistan. Similarly, the cotton textile mills remained mostly in India while the area growing the best-quality cotton went to Pakistan. Production in two of our most important foreign exchange earning industries, viz., jute and cotton textiles, was thus adversely affected by the partition. The evacuation, relief and rehabilitation of millions of people who migrated into India following partition resulted in a refugee problem unparalleled in history and the abnormal expenditure, year after year, on this account intensified the budgetary problem.

This formidable array of problems needed immediate attention from government and a planned utilization of the available meager resources became essential.

There is now a general consensus that unless there is rapid industrialization, India cannot survive—at any rate, as a democracy. When, however, our first Five-year Plan was put forward, it aroused a lot of suspicion in the United States. Many people had then looked upon planning for development as a totalitarian concept. No such planning had been necessary in democratic countries of the West. Why should a plan of development be necessary in a democratic setup like the one in India? It was not appreciated that circumstances were indeed very different. In the case of countries like England and West Europe, the industrial revolution preceded the full development of democracy with universal adult franchise. The industrial revolution was accompanied, at least in the initial stages, by enormous social upheaval, uprooting of large sections of population and subjecting them to untold misery; but the governments, which did not have to depend so much on popular votes, could survive. The hardship and sacrifices were no doubt to some extent mitigated by the exploitation of the resources of the colonies but it was only after political democracy had been fully established, enabling the masses effectively to demand improvement, that a semblance of economic justice could be secured. The newer countries like the U.S.A., Canada and Australia, on the other hand, because of their vast areas, richly endowed with natural resources, could develop through a system of free enterprise without suffering too much from the evils of the industrial revolution. Even so, they needed a century or more to develop despite the very substantial foreign capital that flowed from Britain and other European countries. While the methods followed in these countries and their experiences provide us with valuable lessons, we cannot follow them in their entirety to solve our problems because they are of a different nature. Our political freedom, bringing with it adult franchise, came before the beginning of an industrial revolution. The people naturally demand some improvement in their economic condition; otherwise political independence has no meaning for them. We have therefore to develop our economy in a much shorter time, and at the same time avoid the hardship caused by the industrial revolution in Europe. The methods of rapid growth adopted in the U.S.S.R., Eastern Europe and in China —although some of their problems are similar to those in India—are also of limited interest to us. These methods too have some lessons for us but despite their promise of quick results, they cannot be adopted in a democratic setup. While wishing to benefit from the experience of others, we also like to avoid regimentation, class conflicts, social waste, as well as oppressive concentration of power and wealth. We welcome and, wherever possible, draw upon the ideas, the experience, the advice and assistance of other peoples but the final decision as to the methods most suitable for us must be our own.

It is true that affluent and highly developed societies in the Western world have not found it necessary in the past to plan for development except perhaps in a period of crisis, such as war. They had enough time—many decades—to arrange for high-grade technical training to build up trained manpower on an adequate scale, and to provide for banking and credit facilities for financing both agriculture and industry. We in India have to arrange for training and to develop these facilities for financing both agriculture and industry. We have to arrange for training and to develop these facilities—practically from scratch—in a comparatively much shorter period. We have even to provide our people with basic education, which was sadly neglected during the colonial era. We have to revive our agriculture and industries, which had remained moribund for a long time, to set up new institutions and to introduce new improved methods. All this needs urgent and positive action in a coordinated manner and cannot be left entirely to private enterprise. Our resources are limited while the demands are so varied and numerous. It is necessary to decide on priorities and make suitable allotment of funds. All these requirements can be met only through careful and proper planning so that the scarce capital is not frittered away on less important projects. The plan must provide for first things first, lay the foundation for economic advance and ensure that the limited resources are utilized to the best advantage of the nation. It is unnecessary to elaborate this point further since the need for planning in underdeveloped countries has now been generally recognized. In fact, the pendulum has now swung to the other extreme and today a developing country which has no proper plan finds it difficult to convince donor countries that foreign aid is at all needed, or that if granted, will be used efficiently and to its best advantage. If there is no adequate planning, it is difficult to find out how much local resources would be available and how much could in fact be diverted to social and economic development. For developing countries, planning has thus become an absolute necessity. At the same time, the plan must avoid too much centralization so that enough initiative and opportunities are left to individual or local authorities.

While planning for development is no longer exclusively associated with a totalitarian regime, most Americans still find it difficult to understand why economic development cannot be left to private enterprise or why there should be any need for a public sector in India. These aspects of Indian economic development are still looked upon with suspicion as if they were necessarily totalitarian concepts. It is important to remove these misconceptions. We obtained our political freedom through nonviolent means. We want to achieve our economic freedom equally without violence, injustice or too much social upheaval. At the same time, we cannot afford to wait too long. Indians are a proverbially patient people, but if no tangible improvement can be brought about in a few years' time, their patience might be exhausted. If our efforts to bring about economic and social betterment through democratic means fail, there may be a popular demand to try the alternative—the totalitarian method of development—which already has attraction for some people. It is therefore essential to ensure that our experiment of democratic planning proves to be a success. Having regard to the enormity and the complexity of our problem, we decided to choose a mixed economy incorporating all three methods of economic development which have proved effective in other democratic countries. In our planned development there is therefore room for private enterprise, public enterprise, and also for cooperative enterprise in fields which are specially suited to it such as agriculture and rural industries. New heavy industries and machine tool plants would normally be set up in the public sector. Government would also be responsible for development and expansion of the public utilities, power and transport facilities which are essentially needed to serve other basic industries. With limited resources, private enterprise would either have been unable to finance such gigantic projects or would have been unwilling to take up irrigation projects which would yield no profit for several years. Indian industry is also not sufficiently developed to have surplus technical and managerial staff to organize and administer a rapidly expanding program in the public sector in addition to what it has to do to expand its own program. It is well to remember that for similar reasons, even the highly developed private sector in America, with no shortage of capital, could not be left alone to deal with the development of atomic energy or of the space program. The U. S. Government had to take a hand in both.

The field in which the private sector can function is, however, still a very large one. Private enterprise still produces 90 percent of India's national output. All agriculture is in the private sector. Small and medium industries, as also cottage industries, are entirely in the private sector. Even in heavy industries meant normally for public enterprise, private enterprise continues and expands side by side. Private industries like the Tata Iron and Steel Company, as also the Indian Iron and Steel Company, have nearly doubled their production not only with encouragement but also with substantial assistance from the government. Heavy engineering and construction plants are all in the private sector. Jute and cotton textile industries and the tea industry are entirely in the private sector. The controversy about the public sector is very much exaggerated; in reality one is complementary to the other. The rate of growth in the private sector during the plan period has been very much higher than that in the public sector. Any suspicion that a growth of the public sector stands in the way of the development of the private sector is thus completely unfounded. On the contrary, by taking over the main responsibility of developing power, transport facilities, etc., the government has made it possible for private enterprise to develop many new industries, and promote faster growth in other sectors of our economy.

While one set of people complain that we are too closely following totalitarian methods and drawing up much too ambitious plans, others criticize us for the slower rate of progress in India as compared to that in China. Our plans no doubt appear large in terms of our resources but they are by no means ambitious in relation to our needs. Merely to keep pace with the annual increase in population, even to maintain its existing poor standard of living, India has to make real efforts to go forward. Our struggle to move forward can be compared with the efforts of a man trying to run up a descending escalator. We must struggle hard even if we are to stand still. Without such a struggle we would go backward. For India, time is short and we cannot afford a slower rate of progress. The speed with which improvement is brought about is no less important than the changes themselves.

The criticism about the slower rate of progress in India as compared to that in China is not without substance. One must, however, try to understand the reasons for this difference. Social and economic conditions in India and in China were in many ways comparable. Both had a glorious past, both had become static, had fallen behind Europe in the race for industrialization, and both are now trying to rebuild their respective economies. The difference, however, lies in the method of approach. India wants economic progress and social justice without detriment to the principle of individual freedom and tolerance of different views. Our five-year plans are evolved democratically, at the village level, at the district level, at the state level and finally endorsed by the Indian Parliament. The plan is discussed by different sections of our people and modified in accordance with their wishes, as far as possible. China, on the other hand, has preferred to choose the totalitarian methods of development subordinating the individual to the party and the state.

India is committed to raising its resources by democratic means. In advanced and industrially developed countries, savings available for investment are at least 10 to 15 percent of the national income—sometimes even more. Such substantial savings are possible without depressing the relatively high standards of living. Underdeveloped countries like India which produce little, and have little surplus wealth, consume most of what they are able to produce. The rate of investment is naturally low, seldom exceeding 5 percent of the national income. One way of securing a larger investment would be by deliberately lowering the standard of living and consumption of goods. In a democracy one cannot raise resources by forced contributions or by compulsory delivery of agricultural surpluses to the state. It is possible for a totalitarian government to compel its people to accept a low or static standard of living and thus collect funds for development, by heavy taxes, forced savings and compulsory sale of a large share of crops. Some nations have indeed gone too far in order to achieve spectacular growth even at great human and social cost. The standard of living in India is pitifully low and we have no desire to force it down still lower, nor as a democratic country could we do so. We cannot subject our people to any greater suffering and misery. We must keep the standard of living rising and at the same time draw off as much funds for development as possible.

In a democracy we cannot also force the adoption of new and improved methods without regard to the cost in terms of human life and dignity. We have to follow the more difficult method of persuasion. Each farmer has to be taught, not forced, to use improved methods, better implements, fertilizers and so on. Each craftsman has to be trained so that he can be made to understand how to use new tools and follow modern methods. Even in heavy industries, the introduction of more up-to-date machinery must be so paced that workers are not thrown out without hope of securing new jobs. This is a most important consideration in a country where there is a surplus of labor and unemployment is already at a very high level. The need for technological advance has thus to be balanced against the need for finding employment. No such problem faces the industrially more advanced countries with a high level of employment or countries which are not committed to democratic methods of development. Because of the existence of this problem in India, we have often to make compromises. To find fresh avenues of employment is an important objective in itself and is indeed a social and a political necessity. Labor-saving devices cannot therefore be promptly introduced before finding alternative employment for workers rendered surplus to requirement. Small enterprises and cottage industries employing many, must therefore continue, competing with highly mechanized industries employing a few. That is why we have to allot a substantial quantity of cotton yarns for the employment of our handloom workers. This process of democratic persuasion, cooperation and compromise is naturally slower in yielding results than the totalitarian method of force and coercion.

We have chosen to follow the democratic method of development since that is more in keeping with our history and culture. This method involves consultation and cooperation at all levels from the village right up to the central government and takes note of differing points of view. The reason for adopting this method can be best explained in the words of the late Prime Minister Nehru:

> We have definitely accepted the democratic process.... Because we think that in the final analysis it promotes the growth of human beings and of society; because ... we attach great value to individual freedom and dignity.... We do want high standards of living, but not at the expense of the spirit of man, not at the expense of his creative energy, not at the expense of all those fine things of life which have ennobled man all through the ages.*

By contrast, China has given up such ideals for the sake of achieving a faster development. There is a complete regimentation of men, women and children and the entire people has been forced into service for the government. China has taken full advantage of its huge manpower but in the process has given up any pretense of maintaining even a modicum of human dignity and freedom. The Chinese argument seems to be that, in any case, there never was much civil liberty in China and the denial of what little there may have been makes no difference. It is no use bothering about human dignity when one would otherwise have to go without enough

* Speech to All India Congress Committee, Indore, on January 4, 1957. Reproduced in Jawaharlal Nehru's *Speeches*, Vol. III, page 53.

food and clothing. Human freedom and dignity are luxuries which for the moment can wait. The present generation must be condemned to work like slaves. Then only can the Chinese people hope to make adequate progress—at least in the next generation. It is perhaps on some such considerations that the rural and urban industrial communes in China were left with very little personal freedom or relaxation. Few women can stay at home. Most of them have to work in factories and have little family life. These stringent authoritarian methods are naturally more effective and they do yield quicker results but are not methods which can be adopted under any system of parliamentary democracy. The reasons for the comparatively more rapid development in China are thus clear. Admittedly totalitarian methods are likely to bring about rapid results and imposed methods are more effective than persuasion, at least in the short run. The failure of the Great Leap Forward program in China has, however, now given rise to some doubts in this respect. In any case, we believe that democratic changes are more successful in gaining the acceptance of the people and are thus more enduring from the point of view of final results. We are not therefore prepared to give up the democratic method of development which we have chosen to adopt.

There is a school of thought which believes that India is overpopulated and no matter what is done, there is no hope for the country unless the problem of population is tackled and solved first. It is true that India has a population of 460 million—larger than the combined populations of Africa and South America. The density of population of 383 per square mile still compares favorably with the world's highly populated countries—800 in England and Wales, 782 in Belgium, 909 in Holland, 432 in Italy and 665 in Japan. India's rate of increase in population again is no higher than that in many countries and is lower than that in the South-American countries. The problem however has been acute because India's already vast population is increasing by about 10 million a year. Even so, basically India's problem is not one of overpopulation but one of underproduction. It is not a question of too many people but of too little productivity, both agricultural and industrial. India's greatest potential asset is its large population; its greatest challenge is to utilize their energies and skills to exploit the vast natural resources of the country. At present India is faced with a seeming paradox. On the one hand, there is acute and chronic unemployment and enforced idleness of a large number of people for about five months in the year; on the other hand, there is a severe shortage of trained men and women—doctors, nurses, scientists, engineers, technicians, and skilled workers. We are now trying to remove the anomaly by adapting the Indian education system to the needs of national development and diverting people from white-collar jobs. Attempts are being made to harness our underemployed manpower through community development programs. The results have been most encouraging in every place where there was good leadership.

We realize, of course, that so long as underproduction continues, there can be no substantial increase in the per capita income or an improvement in the standard of living, unless there is an effective curb on the growth of population. The first results of our health programs have been to lower the death rate and to increase life expectancy. We have now to counteract this development by well-organized and widespread efforts at birth control. With a view to control the terrible growth in population, energetic action is being taken to popularize family planning. Birth control clinics have been set up in different parts of the country. India is one of the few countries which is officially supporting a program of birth control. Fortunately, there has been no opposition to this program on religious grounds. Thousands of people have in fact voluntarily gone in for sterilization. It is the abject poverty of the people that stands in the way of their buying contraceptives. The government has now set aside comparatively large funds for their free supply.

There is also considerable ignorance about the treatment of foreign capital in India. We welcome foreign capital, but we wish foreign investors to associate Indian enterprises and capital with themselves. No rigid formula has been laid down prescribing the extent or proportion of foreign participation. Naturally, we prefer that the major proportion of the capital and effective control of the enterprise should remain in Indian hands. In cases where rapid development of an industry is in the national interest and foreign participation is considered essential, exceptions are made and foreign investors are allowed to retain a major interest in ownership and effective control. Foreign investment is however welcome mainly in manufacturing industries, in which Indian enterprise is not yet fully developed. It is also welcome if the produce of these industries helps to augment India's foreign exchange resources either by increasing exports or by reducing imports from foreign countries. Foreign investment is not normally desired in purely trading or financial ventures not involving manufacture. It has been the policy of the Government of India all along to give every facility to foreign investors for remittance of profits and for repatriation of capital. A variety of tax incentives and rebates, tax holiday and a virtual monopoly of the Indian market have been given to attract foreign capital. The fear about the safety and security of the investment is completely unfounded. In fact, President Eisenhower has said, "India is becoming one of the great investment opportunities of our time." It is the policy of the government to encourage the flow of foreign capital in every possible way. If we have not succeeded in attracting substantial private capital the reasons are not due to any unwillingness on our part to have such capital. Foreign investment in India is so small that for a long time we will have no reason to fear such economic domination as is evident in some countries of Europe. President de Gaulle, for example, called for new vigilance against economic domination by the U.S.A. Canada had also at some stage showed some concern on this account. The distrust with which new countries are viewed and ignorance of the opportunities of investment are mainly responsible for the reluctance of private capitalists to invest in distant lands. We welcome private investment so long as it does not go against our economic policy and promotes industrial development in India.

Our per capita income is one of the lowest in the world. Even so, more than 80 percent of our investment in the Indian economy during the plan periods has come from the Indian people themselves. The next few years would be the most crucial period in India's economic history. If the Indian economy is to be given a big enough push so that it can go ahead, expanding and producing more under its own power, it will be necessary to step up the investment on a relatively larger scale. At a time when living standards and the saving potential are already low, we need urgently some measure of foreign capital and assistance in order to cross the takeoff point of economic development. We have set our economy in motion as never before. Acute shortage of foreign exchange, however, stands in the way of importing essential components and raw materials, with the result that even the manufacturing capacity installed often remains unutilized. India's social stability and its future as a democracy depends on the speed with which it pushes ahead the pace of its economic and social growth. What is on trial is whether democracy can solve the problems of mass poverty and unemployment and can bring about a rate of economic progress comparable to what can be achieved by totalitarian methods. Many doubt that problems of such magnitude can be solved through democratic processes, and assert that they cannot in any case be solved fast enough. We in India have faith that the democratic method of development can deliver the goods fast enough. If India can make adequate progress under democracy, it may indeed serve the cause of democracy. In meeting this great challenge to democracy, India hopes to receive the friendly assistance of other nations who share in its belief in the democratic principles of human dignity and individual freedom.

The misconceptions in the United States about Indian economic policy have been partially responsible for much of the criticism that has been made about U.S. aid to India. Some Americans believe that India's policy of nonalignment has in fact worked more often in favor of Communist countries. They therefore do not think that India deserves any aid from the United States when there are so many differences between India and the U.S.A. on important political issues. Another criticism has been that Americans, believing as they do in free enterprise, ought not to assist a country set on having some sort of controlled economy in which the public sector is destined to play an important role. These critics see no difference between the mixed economy chosen by India and some form of state capitalism. On the other hand, the great majority of Americans do not think that an agreement on political issues should be a condition precedent to the granting of aid. They recognize that it is in the American national interest to help in the development of a democratic India. In their view "slavish compliance is a characteristic for which a free society has no use." In his presidential campaign speech on June 14, 1960, President Kennedy had underlined the importance of assisting India's development programs and had then said: "It is vital that we aid India to make a success of her new Five Year program—a success that will enable her to compete with Red China for economic leadership of all Asia, and we must undertake this effort in a spirit of generosity motivated by a desire to help our fellow citizens of the world, not as narrow bankers or self-seeking politicians." It has also been pointed out by many Americans that India qualifies for aid on each one of the grounds on which foreign aid can be justified. If the grounds are humanitarian, if the reason for granting aid is to reduce the grinding poverty, there is hardly any country which is poorer and which is in greater need for help. If the object is to help countries which show the greatest promise of sustained growth and also offer the prospect of developing soon to the takeoff point, India's claims are equally strong. If the object is to open up new markets, India with a population of 460 million—a population larger than that of Africa and South America combined —is potentially one of the most promising markets.

Aid to India has often been sanctioned after heated and sometimes acrimonious discussions in the United States. It is unfortunate that statements of the few who oppose aid hit the headlines in newspapers while those of the many that support it do not get as much publicity and often go unnoticed. Too much importance is given to the criticisms without appreciating that the aid would not have been granted if the majority had not been in its favor. In their annoyance, Indians argue that, after all, the aid is mostly in the form of loans, all of which will have to be repaid with interest, that much of this loan has to be spent in the donor country with resulting increase in its export and that left to ourselves we would have preferred trade to aid. This line of argument ignores how important it is for the receiving country to acquire foreign exchange which cannot otherwise be earned by normal trade and without which further economic development comes to a grinding halt. Americans then complain that there is not enough recognition of the generous economic aid given by the U.S.A. to India. This complaint is not quite justified since American aid receives wide publicity and the extent of the assistance is well known in India. There is thus a vicious circle creating some irritation for no good reason. We should not be oversensitive. We should remember that in a democracy debate is essential and it is not unusual to have heated discussions when the opposition attempts to marshal all possible arguments in support of its views. The democratic processes are also slower. The delay in getting aid approved ought not to be misunderstood, particularly in India where we go through the same process. At the same time, when aid is given after an unpleasant debate the grace is often taken away, even though people may nevertheless express their gratitude for the help they receive.

Many Americans visiting India are struck with the fact that Britain, West Germany and the Soviet Union have received a lot of credit by setting up steel plants which serve as standing monuments to their contributions to Indian economic development. They naturally feel unhappy that although American economic aid has been of a much larger order, there are no similar projects which could be shown as visible symbols of Indo-American collaboration. With a view to removing this anomaly, a proposal was made to secure American collaboration for a large new steel plant at Bokharo. There were protracted and long-drawn-out negotiations, but despite strong support from the American Administration, despite the recommendations of the late President Kennedy himself, the proposal could not get through. India ultimately had to withdraw the request with a view to saving the embarrassment that was being caused to the Administration. It was an open secret that although many criticisms were made, the project fell through not on technical grounds but on the ground that no assistance should be given to this project in the public sector, which, it was wrongly assumed, would compete with private sector steel plants. The Bokharo project is now going to be executed with Soviet technical and financial assistance.

INDIA AND THE
UNITED NATIONS

THE activities of India in the United Nations and its votes on different issues arising in the UN are often cited to create an image of India as hostile toward America. An analysis of the votes cast during the last twelve years from 1952 to 1963 on important political and colonial questions does not, however, bear out the popular belief that India has in general been against the United States or that it has voted more often with the Soviet Union than with the United States. Of the 274 votes on political issues during this period, in 90 cases the United States, the Soviet Union and India voted in the same way. Of the rest, India voted with the United States 62 times and with the Soviet Union 61 times. In the remaining 61 instances, India's vote differed both from that of the U.S.A. and of the USSR. This pattern of voting well reflects the nonaligned position that India has all along taken in the United Nations.

If the statistics are examined a little more closely it will

appear that many of the items on which India and the United
States voted differently are hardy annuals which appear on
the agenda of the United Nations every year. For instance,
one can cite the item on apartheid as practiced in South
Africa. This item has appeared on the agenda of the UN every
year during the period under consideration. For a number of
years the United States used to abstain on resolutions on
apartheid but in later years it changed its policy and began
to vote in favor of the resolution on that subject, thereby
coming around to the position that had been taken all along
by India. In 1962, however, the United States voted against
the resolution, because certain paragraphs of the resolution
by implication called for sanctions against South Africa. Similarly, on the question of China's representation in the UN,
the United States and India have so far always voted differently. Another question which has appeared in almost every
year is the consideration of the report of the UN Commission
for the Unification and Rehabilitation of Korea. On this
question also, India and the U.S.A. often voted differently.
From 1962, however, India changed its attitude and began
to vote in the same way as the U.S.A. The number of times
that India and the U.S.A. did not find it possible to vote in
the same way appears to be fairly large but if one remembers
that many items were considered year after year, the number
of items on which Indian views differed from those of the
United States is very small indeed.

Out of the 71 important votes pertaining to colonial questions, India, the U.S.A. and the USSR voted in the same way
31 times. India voted 22 times in the same way as the USSR
while India and the U.S.A. voted in the same way 11 times.
In the remaining seven cases, India voted independently;
voting neither with the U.S.A. or with the USSR. It is an
unfortunate fact that on colonial issues the Soviet Union

found it easier to go along with the views and aspirations of the Afro-Asian group. In fact, the occasions when India differed on colonial issues with the Soviet Union were those in which the Soviet Union wanted much stronger or more drastic resolutions. If India could not support those resolutions, it was not necessarily because India did not like them but because they were unlikely to command a two-thirds majority. India therefore preferred more moderate resolutions which were assured of success even though they might have fallen short of the desired goal. On the other hand, where a vote of the U.S.A. differed from that of India, it was more often because the United States did not approve of the resolution at all or because it considered that the resolution went too far. The difference in the pattern of voting thus reflects the basic difference in the approach of the U.S.A. and India on colonial issues. During the last few years, however, the United States has shown a much greater inclination to vote on colonial issues in the same way as Asians and Africans.

Even when the U.S.A. and India differed on certain specific issues, the differences were not really as great as were made out at the time. The differences had often been unduly exaggerated. The views of the two countries have, in some cases, come closer together in recent years. Some of the important issues on which India and the U.S.A. expressed divergent views are worth mentioning. One such occasion arose when North Korea invaded South Korea in 1950. India supported the decision that the UN should take action in Korea. India did not, however, agree to send any troops to take part in the fighting. The main reason was that in those early days of our independence, we did not wish to get involved in a war. There was also the belief that if we did not take part in any actual fighting, we might be able to bring about a cease-fire through some formula acceptable to both sides. We did, however, send a medical unit to Korea, much to the annoyance of Peking. India's opposition to the resolution condemning China as an aggressor irritated the Americans. We opposed the resolution because we felt that such a resolution would not only serve no useful purpose but might stand in the way of a negotiated settlement which was then being attempted. Prime Minister Nehru said at the time that it was "our feeling throughout that it was not much good passing resolutions, which, generally speaking, were condemnatory, and associating ourselves with such condemnation even though that condemnation might be justified." * If we had joined in the condemnation, we might not have been able to function as chairman of the Neutral Nations Repatriation Commission that was set up in 1953. Incidentally, our performance in the Commission was appreciated and did a lot to remove the misunderstanding that had been created by Indian votes cast in the UN earlier.

There has often been a complaint that while India reacted sharply and joined in the world outcry against Anglo-French action in Egypt, it did not condemn the Soviet Union for its action in Hungary. This is not quite correct. The Soviet action was as much criticized in India both in the press and in the Parliament. What is true however is that the Government of India was somewhat slower in expressing its views on Hungary. In response to several members' criticism of the Government of India's stand in the UN, Prime Minister Nehru said that India was much more familiar with Egypt in general and the Suez Canal in particular. "The broad facts," he said, "were clear to us and therefore we ventured to express a very clear and definite opinion about them. In regard to Hungary, the difficulty was that the broad facts were not clear

* Debate on Foreign Affairs on December 7, 1950.

to us. Also the occurrences in Hungary took place at a moment when suddenly the international situation became very much worse and we had to be a little surer and clearer as to what had actually happened and what the present position was. Therefore, we were a little cautious in the expression of our opinion in regard to facts though not in regard to general principles that should govern conditions there. As the House knows, right from the very beginning we made it perfectly clear that in regard to Hungary or Egypt or anywhere else, any kind of suppression by violent elements of the freedom of the people was an outrage on liberty. I said that and I made it perfectly clear, first, that foreign forces should be removed both from Egypt and Hungary although the two cases are not parallel; and secondly that the people of Hungary should be given the opportunity to determine their future." *

The situation in Hungary was complicated by the fact that the intervention came from the Soviet Army which was already stationed there and in other East European countries, in accordance with the terms of the Warsaw Treaty. In terms of the Warsaw Pact, the Soviet Army might have had a right to be in Hungary. While we ourselves were strongly in favor of all foreign forces being removed from every country, we had to reckon with the fact that foreign troops were in fact present in NATO countries as well as in Warsaw Pact countries. The situation became even more confusing when attempts were made to use the developments in Hungary "to hide what was happening in Egypt. The struggle in Hungary was represented as the basic thing so as somehow to cover up the misdeeds in Egypt." * * Despite the legalistic arguments and despite the initial confusion as regards the factual posi-

---

* Speech during debate on foreign affairs in Lok Sabha, November 19, 1956.
** Prime Minister Nehru's speech in Lok Sabha on November 19, 1956.

tion, we nevertheless expressed strong views that Soviet forces should be withdrawn from Hungary.

We objected to the resolution calling for elections in Hungary "under UN auspices" because this would have reduced Hungary to less than a sovereign state and as such would have been contrary to the Charter. Such action would have also set up a precedent which might be utilized in future for similar intervention in other sovereign countries.

Americans never could understand how India found it possible to support the "admission" of China to the United Nations, when China was guilty of aggression in Korea and elsewhere and, in American opinion, has all along shown the utmost contempt for the principles of the Charter. They found it still more difficult to understand the Indian attitude when we did not change our views on this question, even after the massive Chinese invasion of India in 1962. The Indian position is that it is quite immaterial whether one likes or dislikes China. This is not a question of "admission" of China to the United Nations. If it were a question of new admission, certainly the American objection would have been valid and we ought not to have supported the admission of a state which does not show any desire to respect the principles of the Charter. The record of China, peaceful or otherwise, would then have been most relevant. One could have rightly opposed the admission to the UN of a country which is undoubtedly guilty of aggression. China is, however, one of the founder members of the United Nations and is a permanent member of the Security Council. In our view, it is merely a question of credentials as to who represents China. Our relations with China today are no doubt strained but that has nothing to do with the basic question of the representation of China. The major problems of the world, including disarmament, cannot unfortunately be dealt with unless Peking is represented in the United Nations. Americans now realize how wrong they were to imagine that once an agreement was reached with the Soviet Union on nuclear testing or on disarmament, the agreement would automatically be acceptable to Peking. The absence of Peking also comes in the way of the functioning of the UN since a substantial area of the world with a large population of six to seven hundred millions is excluded from the United Nations. The solution of the problems that we face today has become even more difficult, and the absence of China from the UN has only added to the complexities of the problems. It may be naïve to assume that Peking would be less inclined to aggression once it was represented in the United Nations but we can only hope that if the Chinese are brought into the United Nations, they may gradually change their outlook under the influence and pressure of world opinion. Many Americans are now veering around to a similar view.

It was a sore point with the U.S.A. when in 1961 India inscribed an item on the agenda regarding the continuation of suspension of nuclear and thermonuclear tests and co-sponsored a resolution calling upon the states concerned to refrain from conducting nuclear explosions pending the conclusion of an internationally binding treaty. The Soviet Union had broken the moratorium and had already resumed atmospheric tests. By some curious logic, the Indian action was interpreted as if it were somehow anti-American and in favor of the Russians. In fact, it was neither anti-American nor pro-Soviet. If the resolution was against anyone, it was more against the Soviet Union which had already resumed these tests. The Americans had not started any testing and admittedly could not start doing so at least for some time since preparation for such tests takes considerable time. If they had not opposed the Indian resolution so vehemently at every stage, the resolution could have been promptly adopted. In that case, it would have been the Soviet Union which would have been seriously embarrassed. They might not have been able to discontinue the series of tests which they had already begun, and the United States could then justify a resumption of their own tests if indeed they so desired. Americans could not have been blamed for not acting up to the resolution if the Russians had already ignored it. Due to American opposition, the Indian resolution was not however adopted until the day when Russians concluded their tests. India was blamed for not having criticized the Soviet Union for resuming the tests. The fact is that the Prime Minister of India, Mr. Nehru, had deplored the resumption of tests by the Soviet Union, even when he was in the Soviet Union as its guest. This fact was not given any publicity in the United States with the result that a wrong impression was created that India was taking a pro-Soviet attitude in this matter.

At a luncheon in New York on November 10, 1961, arranged by the Overseas Press Club and UN Correspondents Association, Mr. Nehru was asked why he did not "clearly condemn Russian renewal of testing." Mr. Nehru in his reply said, "So far as I am concerned, I declared myself quite clearly then and repeatedly on later occasions. I thought it was deplorable that this resumption of nuclear tests should take place." India was also criticized in the U.S.A. as if it wanted only an uncontrolled moratorium. There was no basis for this assumption. Like the U.S.A., India also wanted a prohibition of nuclear tests through an internationally binding agreement under effective international control. Pending the conclusion of such a treaty, however, India continued to press that there should be a complete cessation and prohibition of all kinds of nuclear and thermonuclear tests. India's position was repeatedly explained in the General Assembly but was seldom noticed by the American press. It is significant that within two years the Moscow Treaty was successfully negotiated bilaterally by the U.S. and the USSR putting a ban on all nuclear tests, except those carried out underground.

On questions involving threats to peace, India has on the whole favored the continuance of great power unanimity as the basis of peace-keeping operations. India did not vote positively in favor of the Uniting for Peace Resolution,* which enables the General Assembly to initiate peace-keeping operations when the Security Council is unable to take action because of a lack of great-power unanimity. It is not that India did not realize that it may often be impossible to achieve great-power unanimity, particularly so long as the Cold War continues. At the same time, India could not ignore the realities of the situation, viz., that no action to enforce keeping of the peace can succeed without the willing cooperation of a great power—and more so, if that great power happens to be one of the two superpowers. The great-power veto in the Security Council, in the Indian view, was a recognition by the framers of the Charter, of the facts of life. The right to veto was provided in the Charter as a necessary evil despite the principle of sovereign equality—in theory—of all states. At a time when developed countries were demanding weighted or dual voting in the UN Conference on Trade and Development, it was hardly realistic to deny great-power veto on important political issues. If conciliation procedures are needed to settle differences on economic issues, they are even more necessary on political issues. India believes that any attempt to bypass the provision for great-power veto would only increase tension and that is why India was not in favor of minimizing the effect of great-power veto. Yet once the

* Resolution 377 (V).

Uniting for Peace resolution was adopted, India loyally carried out its collective responsibility, cooperating with others in peace-keeping operations by providing both men and money.

The Indian attitude on the question of the application of Article 19 against the Soviet Union and France and certain other member states which for political reasons found themselves unable to agree to share the cost of UN peace-keeping operations in the Congo and Gaza, has also given rise to much misunderstanding. Here is an instance where no attempt seems to have been made to understand the Indian point of view on this question. Our attitude was considered to be anti-American and even unworthy motives were imputed. Warren Unna writing in the Washington *Post* on October 15, 1964, went to the extent of saying that "there was also speculation that India, having just been promised new military assistance in Moscow, might be making a down payment in kind." The absurdity of this imputation would have been apparent to anyone if only he had taken the trouble of looking up the records in the UN two years earlier when we voted in favor of accepting the advisory opinion of the International Court of Justice. It had then been made clear that we accepted the opinion mainly on the consideration that "the dignity of the Court should be maintained and its advisory opinion merited the respect which had never previously been denied to such opinions." In our statement made at the time, we had said, "The advisory opinion did not mean that Article 19 of the Charter would automatically come into operation or even that it had any relevance to an Assembly decision to accept the opinion. The advisory opinion merely established the legal position on a specific issue; no action automatically flowed from it. Considerations that were not legal might be equally valid and must influence the Assembly in determining its ultimate course of action." * It may be recalled that in December 1962, when the statement was made, there was no occasion for India to be specially grateful to the Soviet Union. In the wake of the Chinese attack on India, Mr. Khrushchev, while taking a neutral stand as between India and China, had shown some partiality for China when he said, "Indians are our friends, Chinese are our brothers and allies." On the other hand, an immense fund of goodwill had then been created toward the United States of America for its prompt response to our urgent appeal for military help. Even so, we had made these specific reservations regarding the application of Article 19. One would have had to be a clairvoyant to perceive, two years earlier, that the Soviet Union would also in 1964 promise some military assistance to India!

We have repeatedly made clear the reasons why we could not support the application of Article 19 in these cases. We ourselves had paid our full contributions and had supported peace-keeping operations with men, material and money, despite the Soviet view that these peace-keeping operations were irregular. We did not accept that view. On the contrary, we tried to convert others to our point of view. We accepted the advisory opinion of the Court and we also voted in favor of the assessments made by the General Assembly. By doing so, we exerted the maximum pressure on member states that were unwilling to make any contributions toward the cost of peace-keeping operations. Our hope that under all this pressure they might acquiesce in making some payments did not materialize. There was nothing more we could do by way of persuasion. The issue was not merely financial as the Americans had at first argued, but was primarily a political one, as was later recognized by all. Legal considerations are

* 972nd meeting of the Fifth Committee held on December 12, 1962.

no doubt important but the General Assembly is a political body and had to examine this basically political question more from that point of view. In the Indian view, political and other considerations well outweighed the purely legal aspects of the case. We realized that if the Assembly decided to apply Article 19, all that would happen would be that the member states concerned would lose their vote but the financial difficulties of the United Nations would be no nearer solution. We would merely create an additional problem—a political problem. If so many countries lost their votes and among them happened to be two great powers—the Soviet Union and France—who are permanent members of the Security Council, the United Nations would have been seriously weakened and would have lost its representative character. It was in these circumstances, when the very existence of the organization was in danger, that we felt we must admit our failure to force the will of the majority on the minority and work for a compromise.

The American attitude was that once the General Assembly had initiated a peace-keeping operation, and once the International Court of Justice had given its advisory opinion that the expenditures incurred were expenses of the organization within the meaning of Article 17 of the Charter, every member state must be made to pay its assessed share or else lose its right to vote under Article 19 of the Charter. The will of the majority must prevail. The fact was ignored that the great powers in general, and the two superpowers in particular, have interest in practically all problems of the world, but their interests are not necessarily the same and in fact they are very divergent and often conflicting. When a peace-keeping operation is undertaken, this difference in interest—rightly or wrongly—is reflected in the willingness of the country concerned to share the costs of that particular operation.

In the present cases it was the Soviet Union and France which were isolated, but in some other case in the future it may well be the U.S.A. which would be in a similar position. It is best to recognize the realities and not attempt to force the will of the majority on the minority, particularly when there is at present no means of enforcing a majority decision on a great power. We must recognize that we have not yet been able to evolve a world government and the member states have not surrendered their sovereignty beyond what they have agreed to do by subscribing to the Charter of the UN. We must of course try to persuade member states to surrender sovereignty to a still greater extent, but we can succeed in such efforts only when every state agrees. However much we may want every member state to join in a UN peace-keeping operation, we have to recognize the hard fact that this ideal can not be achieved so long as there is no end of the Cold War and there is a clash of interests.

The Indian view that we cannot force any member state to contribute toward the cost of peace-keeping operations undertaken by the General Assembly is by no means a new or a novel one as the Americans seem to contend. In adopting the Uniting for Peace Resolution, the General Assembly had also established a Collective Measures Committee with a mandate to report on the methods which might be used to maintain and strengthen international peace and security. The Collective Measures Committee was composed of Australia, Belgium, Brazil, Burma, Canada, Egypt, France, Mexico, the Philippines, Turkey, the United Kingdom, the U.S.A. and Venezuela. After two years of hard work, the Committee came to the conclusion that although the ideal should be to have "the widest possible participation" in peace-keeping operations, it nevertheless recognized that complete unanimity was not attainable. The Committee therefore recommended that the economic and financial measures should "be equitably shared as far as possible among the cooperating States"—not all states. If there was any doubt that this recommendation regarding equitable sharing did not refer to the financial cost of the operation, all doubts were removed and the position was made quite clear in the second report of the Collective Measures Committee submitted to the VII Session of the General Assembly. The Committee then suggested * "that the Security Council or the General Assembly should establish an ad hoc negotiating committee to deal directly with the States in respect of their contributions." It stated further that "the basic purpose of the ad hoc committee would be to obtain for the United Nations, the forces, manpower, assistance, facilities, services and *funds* required for the effective conduct of the military operations." The Committee was realistic enough to recognize the fact that member states could not be compelled to contribute to peace-keeping operations against their will and that negotiations would be needed to persuade each state to make equitable contributions. If there are some states which refuse to contribute, the burden would have to be equitably shared among the cooperating states. It is clear that in adopting the Uniting for Peace Resolution the member states, at least contemporaneously, did not envisage that unwilling countries should be compelled to pay their share of the cost of peace-keeping operations.

The Committee as constituted was by no means anti-American and at any rate was not pro-Soviet. It is therefore hardly fair to criticize India for making a similar proposal, namely, that the contributions cannot be made compulsory. It is still less fair to attribute motives. With the Cold War still on,

* Supplement No. 17/A/2215.

India is unwilling to take any action which, though otherwise desirable, may, because of lack of great-power unanimity, threaten to break up the organization. When any proposal imperils the very existence of the organization, India has not hesitated to oppose that proposal, no matter where it may originate from. Soviet desire to get rid of Hammarskjöld in 1960 was not supported, and its proposal to set up a Troika was firmly rejected by India, as it was recognized that such actions might wreck the organization.

India's votes in the UN have also sometimes differed from those of the United States on a few economic questions as well. The reasons for this difference are not far to seek. The attitude of the U.S.A., the richest and the economically most developed country in the world, on such questions must necessarily be different from that of an underdeveloped and poor country like India. The fact that such differences have arisen only on rare occasions is a tribute to the capacity of one country to adjust its own requirements to those of the other.

Despite the apparently widespread belief in the United States to the contrary, a scrutiny of the voting in the UN shows that apart from racial and colonial issues, India's position on important political questions has been closer to the American rather than to the Soviet position. In fact, it is one of the Soviet complaints against India, that despite Soviet support of India on issues of vital interest to it, India has not given as much support to issues of interest to the Soviet Union. Such complaints both from the U.S.A. and the USSR will appear only natural if one remembers that India follows a policy of nonalignment—a policy which requires a consideration of each issue on its merits as they appear to India. India may be right or wrong in its judgment. Naturally, Indian views will sometimes agree with one great power or the other and sometimes they will agree with neither. If the reasons for the difference in the pattern of voting is understood, there would then be no cause for misunderstanding or for a feeling that India is hostile to the USA. Friendship does not require agreement at all times and on all issues. Friends can and often do agree to differ. It is well to remember what President Truman had once said about the newly emerging countries: "We must not act as though we wished to degrade them to the rank of satellites by exacting a rigid and humiliating subservience which no free nation could with dignity accept. We will never be defeated as long as we truly stand for a free partnership of free peoples. The unconquerable power of the free world lies in the fact that loyalties are not coerced." * It would be a tragic mistake to ignore this sound advice.

* March 6, 1952, to Congress. Department of State Bulletin, Vol. XXVI, No. 664, pages 403–404.

PARTITION OF INDIA

W E have so far examined some aspects of the foreign and economic policies of India as also Indian activities in the UN which have either been considered unfriendly or have been misunderstood in the U.S.A. As far as Indians are concerned, nothing has subjected Indo-American relations to greater strain than the American attitude on Kashmir and military alliance with Pakistan. The American attitude on Kashmir is based on a number of misconceptions. In the back of their minds Americans have the erroneous belief that British India was partitioned into two independent countries, Hindu India and Moslem Pakistan. It seems to them therefore somewhat logical that Kashmir with a Moslem majority should go to Moslem Pakistan. Such reasoning may have the merit of simplicity, but the statement is not factually quite correct; nor is the problem that simple. For one thing, India still has some fifty million Moslem citizens. With some thirty more millions of its citizens professing other faiths,

India can hardly be described as a Hindu state. In any case, India has chosen to remain a secular state. Pakistan has of course made Islam the state religion and calls itself the Islamic Republic of Pakistan. A brief reference to the more recent history of British India leading up to its partition is perhaps necessary for a proper understanding of the problem.

British historians have drawn a picture of deep-seated Hindu-Moslem conflict starting from the earliest days of Moslem conquest of India. It is true that some Moslem rulers had been intolerant, cruel and fanatical; it is equally true that others had been outstandingly liberal and progressive in their outlook. On the whole, it would not perhaps be wrong to say that the Moslem kings and rulers of India were no worse than their contemporaries in Europe. In fact religious persecution in India when it did take place under Moslem rule was perhaps no more severe than what we hear of the Spanish Inquisition. There were of course conversions forcible or otherwise but by and large the two communities coexisted side by side for nearly a thousand years. The rulers fought among one another—not necessarily on the basis of religion—but the people were hardly affected by reason of their religion. The Moghul Army not only recruited both Hindus and Moslems, but many of the generals commanding these armies came from among the Hindu princes of Rajputana. The internecine wars that went on were seldom if ever fought on communal lines. On the contrary, the wars were mostly fought on considerations of regional interest and sometimes because of clash of personalities. Moslem rulers of South India had a predominantly Hindu army, while the great Maratha rulers who fought against the Moghul emperors had many of their gunners from the Moslem community. The Nawab of Bengal was betrayed by his Moslem commander-in-chief when he fought Clive, but not by his Hindu officers. Hindus and

Moslems often fought jointly against the British. It would not therefore be entirely correct to say that the Hindu-Moslem conflict was a constant feature throughout the Moslem period of Indian history or that partition of the country was inherent in the circumstances of India.

It would be equally wrong to put the entire responsibility for the partition of India on the British Government. The British must, however, bear a large share of the blame for encouraging and developing separatist tendencies among the Moslems of India. During the long period of British rule in India, the rulers not only made no attempt at reconciliation or national integration but encouraged divisive forces in every possible manner. During the first few decades of British rule in India Moslems, for a variety of reasons, refused to go in for Western education. They therefore remained backward and the Hindus, who took more readily to Western methods of training, forged ahead of the Moslems. The British rulers naturally preferred the English-educated Hindu to the less Western-oriented Moslem. Hindus almost monopolized all avenues of employment that were generally being opened to Indians. As more and more Hindus received Western education, more and more of them were imbued with Western ideals of freedom and democracy. Hindus became more and more vocal in demanding freedom and the introduction of parliamentary democracy in India. Such demands only made them suspect in the eyes of the British administrator, whose friendliness for the Hindu changed to antipathy toward him. As demands for political rights increased, the British interest in the Hindu intelligentsia waned and their interest in the Moslem increased. When local self-government was introduced in the eighties of the last century at the instance of the progressive Governor-General Lord Ripon, the Moslems demanded and succeeded in obtaining nominations to local and district boards, even though other seats had to be filled by election. The demands went up further when the next dose of reforms was introduced. The partition of Bengal, which gave an impetus to the growth of nationalist movements all over India, embarrassed the British Government in India. Lord Morley, the then British Secretary of State for India, came out with his famous statement, "Rally the minorities."

The most important single factor responsible for the creation of communal ill-feeling in India was the unfortunate decision, in 1909, of the British Government to introduce the principle of communal electorates, as also the principle of weighted representation for the Moslems. The Moslem community was granted representation beyond its numerical strength. It was in furtherance of this policy that the seeds of communal discord were sown in the Morley-Minto Reforms of 1909. Two separate electorates were introduced—one for the Moslems and the other for the rest of the communities, Hindus, Christians, Buddhists, etc. In accordance with that decision of the British Government, Moslem candidates could get elected only with the votes of the Moslem electorate. This separation of Moslem voters from the rest of the electorate comprising the Hindu majority as also the other minorities such as Christians, Buddhists, Sikhs and the Parsis inevitably led to the gradual development of a feeling of separatism among one section of Moslems, who later formed the Moslem League. Even so, liberal and nationalist Moslems still preferred to join the Indian National Congress Party because it was a noncommunal party and was open to all sections of the community. It is this policy of separatism introduced and encouraged by the British colonial rulers which was responsible for dividing the communities. From that time onward, the communities fell farther and farther apart. The Moslem found that it paid to be communal in one's outlook. The more communal he showed himself to be, the greater was his chance of getting elected from a purely Moslem electorate. Moslems insisted on and got away with communal representation in government services, communal representation in local bodies and communal representation in legislative assemblies. Reservation of seats for Moslems might have been justified for the protection of their legitimate interests, but the British Government went beyond that objective when it insisted that the Moslem representatives to the legislature must also be elected by a separate Moslem electorate. This was really the beginning of an active policy of "divide and rule." The British of course do not admit that they followed any such policy. Their object, they say, was only to protect the legitimate interests of a minority community. The cry "Rally the minorities" and the creation of a separate communal electorate cannot however be explained on such a theory. Nor can one explain on this theory why none of the other religious communities, Christians, Buddhists, Sikhs or Parsis, though they were far less numerous than Moslems, could get separate electorates and why they were all lumped with the large majority of Hindus so far as the electorate was concerned. They needed protection much more than Moslems, if indeed any protection was needed.

In 1919 when the next dose of reforms was being considered, even many prominent Moslems expressed their opposition to separate communal electorates. No less a person than Mr. Mohammed Ali Jinnah who represented the Moslem League before the Joint Select Committee of the House of Lords and the House of Commons, even under persistent cross-examination, adhered to his view that separate communal electorates should be abolished.* Despite the expression of such views, even by some Moslem leaders, communal electorates were once again thrust upon us. Communal electorates were once again retained in the Government of India Act of 1935, driving the Moslem communities farther and farther apart from other communities. It is this poisonous seed which sprouted later into the two-nation theory of the Moslem League that Hindus and Moslems are two different nations, and culminated in the partition of British India and the creation of Pakistan as a separate state.

India rejected the pernicious two-nation theory enunciated by the Moslem League, but we accepted the partition, making it possible for certain contiguous Moslem majority areas in the former British India to secede and constitute a separate Dominion of Pakistan. Since the Moslem League would under no circumstances agree to the emergence of a united free India, partition had to be accepted. It was obvious that the independence of India would otherwise be delayed. Partition was the price we had to pay for our own independence. It was also hoped that once partition of British India was agreed to, there would no longer be any occasion for the Moslem League to continue its campaign of hate and that the relations between the two countries would become cordial as befits two neighbors, if only under the compulsions of history and geography. That hope has been belied. Pakistanis say that Indians have not yet been reconciled to the partition. We can only repeat that we accept the partition as a settled fact. What is, however, true is that we cannot, and never did, accept the theory that Moslems and Hindus are two separate nations, for if we accept that proposition, fifty million Indian

* Report of the Joint Select Committee on the Government of India Bill, Volume II, page 225.

Moslems would become aliens through no fault of theirs. No nation can survive with such a large alien population. That could only mean the ultimate disintegration of India.

It would be a mistake to think that this demand for communal electorates and communal representation in government services was prompted by religious fanaticism. On the contrary, these demands were made mostly by the Western-oriented Moslem leaders. They could of course easily rouse the fanaticism that was latent among the ignorant and illiterate masses of the population. The growing communal conflict can, however, be attributed more to a struggle for political and economic power than to religious differences. It was a clash of vested interests. The majority community, by reason of its better education and training, and also because of its greater wealth, was confident that it would always be able to claim its rights as a majority. Moslems, on the other hand, felt, precisely for these reasons, that they must have special protection to ensure not only what was due to them but also to secure a weighted representation. When the educated Moslem found that by claiming special privileges as a Moslem he could be assured of better prospects in life—prospects which he could not secure in competition with better-qualified candidates—he had no interest in remaining above communalism. It is ironical that the weighted representation in services that the Moslem League insisted on, before independence, has been denied to East Pakistanis, who cannot secure adequate representation in the higher services through competitive examinations. The reason given is that any such special representation would lower the efficiency of the services. When similar arguments were advanced against special representation of Moslems in British India, the Moslem League of course rejected them. Many Moslems who had previously joined the Indian Congress Party saw that numerous special privileges could be claimed as Moslems and gradually started breaking away from the Congress and joining the communal Moslem League Party. The Moslem League claimed to be the sole representative of the Moslems of India and ultimately claimed to be a separate nation. No safeguards could satisfy them even though the Congress Party was prepared to go to almost any length to meet Moslem demands for protection. This attitude of the League gave rise to the quip: "The League had a difficulty for every solution." In fact, it is because of this struggle for power between the two major communities that the British rule could go on in India so long. In the mass movements launched by the Congress in its struggle for independence, the Moslem League remained singularly aloof. In fact, very often it sided with the British in the struggle between the Congress and the British Government. It was therefore but natural that most British administrators in India were well disposed toward the Moslem League. After all, the Indian National Congress was giving so much trouble to them. The Congress Party, while prepared to concede all reasonable demands for protection of the minority, would not agree that Indian Moslems who were ethnically, culturally and linguistically the same as other Indians could constitute a separate nation. The contention of the Congress was that India was one even though its people owed allegiance to different religions. Religion by itself could never be the basis of nationality. The Indian National Congress wanted to have a united secular India against the Moslem League demand for a separate Islamic State of Pakistan. It is this basic conflict in ideology that has revealed itself in the Kashmir dispute, which is essentially a continuation of this old clash of the concepts of a secular state and a religious state. The Moslem League's main platform was one of antagonism toward the Indian National Congress. It is true that in the last days of British rule in India, some liberal-minded British politicians tried to resist the Moslem League's demand for a separate state and made some honest efforts to avoid a partition. Their efforts were foredoomed to failure. The policy actively pursued during the last half century of the British rule had succeeded too well in developing strong separatist feelings which could no longer be controlled. When it became impossible to continue British rule any longer, the policy of "divide and rule" led inexorably to the logical end, divide and quit. The unity of India, which the British rightly claimed to be their greatest achievement, had to be sacrificed.

On the face of it, India and Pakistan have more in common than any two other countries in the world. This is but natural. We have had the same background. We have inherited the same composite culture of India. We speak the same languages and it is difficult to distinguish an Indian from a Pakistani or vice versa. We are ethnically the same people. We have a common history, and geographically the entire subcontinent of India and Pakistan constitutes a natural unit. Paradoxical as it may seem, it is perhaps this very similarity of the two people that has driven them farther and farther apart. When the leaders of the old Moslem League decided to carve a separate state out of what was then British India, their main problem was how to sustain a separate identity in the midst of so much similarity. To make matters even more difficult, the western wing of Pakistan was separated from the eastern wing by nearly a thousand miles of Indian territory. Except the ties of Islam, there is nothing to bind the two wings together. They differ from each other not only in language but also in their ethnic origin. They dress differently and their food habits are different. East Pakistan found more in common with the adjoining Indian province of West Bengal than with West Pakistan. It was not easy to knit the two wings together. The leaders of Pakistan thought that the only way of bringing the two wings closer and at the same time preserve their separate identity was by developing a common antipathy toward India. The internal conflict that existed between the Moslem League and the Indian National Congress was translated into an international conflict between India and Pakistan. Even after partition, India was anxious to keep intact the economic, cultural and social contacts with Pakistan. Pakistan, however, broke up the normal trade relations. Before partition, raw cotton grown in an area that is now Pakistan used to feed the textile mills situated in parts which are now in India. Similar was the position with regard to the jute mills of Calcutta which received their supplies of raw jute from East Pakistan. After independence, Pakistan decided to export raw cotton and jute to other countries, making it necessary for India to import cotton from distant countries and to grow jute in other parts of India even though it was at first uneconomical to do so. For the sake of keeping up cultural and social contacts, India had always advocated complete freedom of movement of the people of the two countries. We had hoped that the Indo-Pakistan frontier would be kept as free as the frontier between Canada and the United States of America. It was at the insistence of Pakistan that we had to agree to introduce the passport and visa system for travel between India and Pakistan.

A feeling seems to have grown up among the Pakistani leaders that Pakistan must always follow a course different from that of India. The history of the foreign policy of Pakistan has been a story of an intensive search for friends and allies against India. To start with, Pakistan, like India, was committed to a policy of noninvolvement in the Cold War.

Both adopted a parliamentary system of government. On August 16, 1947, Prime Minister Liaquat Ali Khan made a policy statement and said:

"I wish it to be clearly known abroad that Pakistan starts on its career without any narrow and special commitments and without any prejudices in the international sphere. Whatever conflict of ideologies there may be between certain other nations, Pakistan is not concerned with them and will take no sides. We believe that the world is large enough to provide scope for the full play of conflicting ideologies and ways of life, without creating international conflicts across territorial frontiers." *

Soon after, Pakistan chose to give up the policy of nonalignment mainly as a counter to India's policy of nonalignment. In the height of the Cold War, Pakistan joined the Western bloc. With the thawing in the Cold War and with the deterioration in Sino-Indian relations, Pakistan turned to the People's Republic of China for sympathy and support in its own quarrels with India. When the Chinese attacked India in the autumn of 1962, if there had been the slightest sympathy from Pakistan, there would have been a wave of goodwill for Pakistan all over India. Not only did Pakistan show no sympathy, it went all out to show its hostility to India in its hour of peril. India's difficulty was Pakistan's opportunity, said a section of the Pakistani press. It was not China but India which was responsible for the conflict, said some Pakistani leaders. Another campaign of hate was let loose. Every effort was made to stop any military aid coming to India. When these efforts did not altogether succeed, relations with its allies cooled off. Pakistan then developed the warmest and the friendliest relations with the People's Re-

* *Dawn,* Karachi, August 18, 1947.

public of China. All this change in its policy has not been dictated by any political principle unless it is one of hostility to India. The disputes between India and Pakistan—including that over Kashmir—have to be viewed against this background.

KASHMIR

BEFORE independence, the subcontinent of India consisted of British India which was directly administered by the British and some 565 Indian princely states which were quasi-independent, ruled by Indian princes, completely autonomous in internal affairs, but owing suzerainty to the British Crown. During our negotiations with the British Government for independence, a demand was made that certain contiguous territories in British India with a Moslem majority must be allowed to secede from the rest of India to constitute a new Dominion of Pakistan. This demand was conceded by the British Government with the agreement of the two principal political parties in India, viz., the Indian National Congress and the Moslem League. The question of the future of the Indian princely states after the withdrawal of the British from the subcontinent was then considered. The British Government had made it quite clear that the partition that created Pakistan was to be confined to the region that constituted the territories of former British India and that this principle did not apply to the Indian states, such as Kashmir, which were ruled by Indian princes. This would be clear from the British Government's announcement of June 3, 1947, which said:

> His Majesty's Government wish to make it clear that the decisions announced [about partition] ... refer only to British India, and that their policy towards Indian States contained in the Cabinet Mission's Memorandum of 12th May, 1946, remains unchanged.

The Cabinet Mission's memorandum reads as follows:

> His Majesty's Government will cease to exercise the power of paramountcy. This means that the rights which flow from the relationship to the Crown will not longer exist, and that all the rights surrendered by the State to the Paramount power will return to the State.
>
> Politically, arrangements between the State on the one side and the British Crown on the other will thus be brought to an end. The void will have to be filled either by the States entering into a federal relationship with the successor Government or Governments in British India, or, failing this, enter into particular political arrangements with it or them.

The British Government thus made it clear that on its withdrawal from India, the suzerainty of the British Crown would lapse, leaving the princes completely free to accede to either the Dominion of India or the Dominion of Pakistan or to make some alternative arrangement with either of them. Section 2 (4) of the Indian Independence Act of 1947 permitted the accession of Indian states to either dominion. The procedure for accession to either dominion was laid down in the Government of India Act of 1935. Both these Acts were Acts of the British Parliament. The ruler of the princely state was given the right to sign a document of accession on behalf of his state, and the Governor-General as the head of the dominion concerned was specified as the authority competent to accept this document. Provision for accession was made in the Government of India Act of 1935 as amended under the Indian Independence Act of 1947 in the following words:

> An Indian State shall be deemed to have acceded to the Dominion if the Governor General has signified his acceptance of an Instrument of Accession executed by the Ruler thereof.

The law regarding accession is thus clear. There was no suggestion that any other action was necessary to make the accession final. There was no requirement for ascertaining popular will on either side; neither the people of the Indian princely state nor the people of the dominion concerned had any say in this matter of accession. Nor was there any provision for a conditional or temporary accession. An accession once made was complete and final. An eminent constitutional expert, Professor A. B. Keith, had as early as November 26, 1934, warned the Indian princes to think long before they committed themselves to such an indissoluble federation. The accession, as such, had to be made by the ruler of the state to the Governor-General of the dominion concerned, who as a constitutional head could, of course, only act on the advice of his cabinet. The fact remains, however, that neither the people of the state nor the people of the dominion concerned came into the picture in any way. Right or wrong, this was the procedure laid down for accession.

This procedure was followed in regard to all the Indian princely states and the rulers of these states acceded in accordance with this procedure either to India or to Pakistan. Legally and constitutionally nothing more was needed. Unlike most other rulers who had acceded either to India or to

Pakistan before August 15, 1947—the day of independence —the ruler of Kashmir did not make up his mind in regard to accession. Pending a decision on accession, he asked for a Standstill Agreement both with India and with Pakistan in regard to communications, supplies and post and telegraph arrangements which had always been interlinked with British India. The Government of Pakistan concluded a Standstill Agreement with the ruler of Kashmir, but before a similar Standstill Agreement with India could be concluded, tribal raids started. Despite the conclusion of the Standstill Agreement, Pakistan cut off communications and stopped supplies of essential commodities and thereby put stringent economic pressure on Kashmir to accede to Pakistan. When this economic pressure failed, armed invasion by tribesmen and other nationals of Pakistan followed. The appeals of the ruler of Kashmir to Pakistan to control its nationals and stop the raids were of no avail. The Kashmir state troops which were deployed along the western border had been split up into small isolated groups and were incapable of offering effective resistance to such a large body of raiders.

Events moved fast, the raiders made rapid advances and the threat to the valley of Kashmir became grave. Unable to prevent raiders from committing large-scale killings, arson, plunder and rape, the ruler of Kashmir urgently appealed to the Government of India on October 26, 1947, for military help and requested that the Jammu and Kashmir State should be allowed to accede to the Dominion of India. An appeal for help was also simultaneously received by the Government of India from the National Conference, the largest political organization in Kashmir. The National Conference, which was predominantly Moslem, also supported the request for the state's accession to India. The Government of India was thus approached not only officially by the ruler but also on behalf of the people of Kashmir, for military aid and for the accession of the state to India. Lord Mountbatten, the then Governor-General of India, accepted the document of Accession. Once Kashmir acceded to India, it became an integral part of India. Thereafter, it was both the right and the obligation of India to send troops to Kashmir for the protection of the people of Kashmir against the tribal invasion and to put a stop to the atrocities that were being committed by the raiders. This is how India came to be in Kashmir.

On December 22, 1947, in Delhi, the Prime Minister of India handed over to the Prime Minister of Pakistan a letter requesting the Government of Pakistan to deny to raiders:

(a) all access and use of Pakistan territories for operation against Kashmir;
(b) all military and other supplies; and,
(c) all other kinds of aid that might tend to prolong the struggle.

On December 30, 1947, the Prime Minister of Pakistan replied as follows:

As regards the charges of aid and assistance to the invaders, by the Pakistan Government, we emphatically repudiate them. On the contrary, the Pakistan Government have continued to do all in their power to discourage the tribal movements by all means, short of war.

On January 1, 1948, India brought the case to the Security Council. In its letter, the Government of India invited a reference to Article 35 of the Charter and said:

Such a situation now exists between India and Pakistan owing to the aid which invaders consisting of nationals of Pakistan and of tribesmen from the territory immediately adjoining Pakistan on the North West, are drawing from

Pakistan for operations in Jammu and Kashmir.... The Government of India request the Security Council to call upon Pakistan to put an end immediately to the giving of such assistance which is an act of aggression against India.

In that same letter, the Security Council was also requested to ask the Government of Pakistan:

(i) to prevent Pakistan government personnel, military and civil, participating in or assisting the invasion of Jammu and Kashmir State;

(ii) to call upon other Pakistani nationals to desist from taking any part in the fighting in the Jammu and Kashmir State; and,

(iii) to deny to the invaders:
   (a) access to and use of its territory for operations against Kashmir;
   (b) military and other supplies; and
   (c) all other kinds of aid that might tend to prolong the present struggle.

The fact that is often forgotten is that it was India that had brought the situation in Kashmir to the attention of the Security Council and these were the reliefs that we had asked for.

In his reply dated 15th January, 1948, the Foreign Minister of Pakistan said:

The Pakistan Government emphatically deny that they are giving aid and assistance to the so-called invaders or have committed any act of aggression against India. On the contrary, and solely with the object of maintaining friendly relations between the two countries, the Pakistan Government have continued to do all in their power to discourage the tribal movements by all means short of war. The allegation made by the Indian Government that the Pakistan Government has afforded aid and assistance to Azad Kashmir forces or that these forces have bases in Pakistan territory or that these forces are being trained by Pakistan officers or are being supplied with arms and materials by the Pakistan Government, is utterly unfounded.

This was a total and straight denial of our allegations and it confirmed what the Prime Minister of Pakistan had already stated on December 30, 1947. It is significant that at this stage Pakistan never tried to justify its presence in Kashmir or to claim any right to be there. Pakistan was obviously quite aware of the fact that its presence in Kashmir was contrary to international law and it was fully conscious of the illegality of its action. That is why Pakistan could not admit its presence in Kashmir and that is why there was a total and straight denial to our complaint. At the time, it did not perhaps occur to the Pakistanis that by denying their presence in Kashmir and by making a categorical statement that Pakistan had no hand in the invasion of Kashmir, they might find it most inconvenient later on to explain how and why they came to be in Kashmir at all. They could not very well talk on behalf of the tribesmen if they had nothing to do with them. That is why Pakistan later admitted its presence in Kashmir.

At the meeting of the Security Council on January 17, 1948, Sir Mohammad Zafurullah Khan, the then Foreign Minister of Pakistan, reiterated that his government had no knowledge with regard to what was actually happening inside the Kashmir State except so far as the reports that had appeared in the press or communications that had been directly addressed to his government. Yet, according to Father Shanks of St. Joseph's Convent in Baramullah, Cunningham, the then Governor of North-West Frontier Province of Pakistan had sent troops to Baramullah to rescue him and his party. It does seem most unlikely that the Governor of the N.W.F.P. could know even the precise location of the raiders on a particular day, and that the Central Government of Pakistan was totally ignorant of what was going on.

In its long reply of January 15, 1948, Pakistan had made a number of countercomplaints unconnected with the complaint of India relating to Kashmir. These countercomplaints referred to other matters which in the opinion of the Pakistan Government had been poisoning the relationship between the two countries. The only countercomplaint made by Pakistan which is relevant to the Indian case on Kashmir was that:

> India obtained the accession of the State of Jammu and Kashmir by fraud and violence.

Pakistan could not produce any evidence in support of this allegation. India had never put any pressure on the ruler of Kashmir to accede to India. In fact, Lord Mountbatten, the then Governor-General of India, had told the ruler on behalf of the government that he might accede to Pakistan if he so wished and that we would not take it as an unfriendly act. This advice was given in the hope that the ruler would soon make up his mind and would not leave the future of the state uncertain, thereby making it a center of conflict and intrigue, specially in a frontier area. At that time a British general was Commander-in-Chief of the Indian Army, and a British air marshal was commanding our Air Forces. The minutes of these officials are on our official records and they clearly prove that there was not even talk of India intervening in Kashmir, militarily. The possibility that the ruler of Kashmir might ask for Indian help was considered for the first time only two days before the actual accession. Not one Indian national was sent to fight in Kashmir before the date of accession. There can thus be no question of any fraud or of violence or even of a threat of violence on the part of India to induce the ruler of Kashmir to accede to India. There was, of course, violence from the Pakistani side and if it is implied that the ruler of Kashmir acceded to India not freely, not of his own volition, but under pressure of circumstances then prevailing, then one must point out that the circumstances were the creation of Pakistan. Surely, Pakistanis cannot be permitted to make a grievance of circumstances for which they alone were responsible.

Pakistan has no legal status in Kashmir. It was only through an act of aggression that it could get into Kashmir. Pakistan was not invited either by the ruler or by the people of Kashmir. It was not as if Pakistan was not aware of the position of Indian princely states after the withdrawal of the British from India. This is what Mr. Jinnah, the founder of Pakistan, had said on June 17, 1947:

> Constitutionally and legally the Indian States will be independent sovereign States on the termination of paramountcy and they will be free to decide for themselves to adopt any course they like; it is open to them to join the Hindusthan [Indian] Constituent Assembly or the Pakistan Constituent Assembly or to decide to remain independent. . . .
> The policy of the All India Muslim League has been clear from the very beginning. We do not wish to interfere with the internal affairs of any State. That is a matter primarily to be resolved between the rulers and peoples of the State.*

At that time Mr. Jinnah did not think that the states must join Pakistan if the majority of the population happened to be Moslem. He was prepared to give the states complete freedom to accede to India or to Pakistan or even to remain independent. According to Mr. Jinnah, until its accession to India,

* *Times* of India, Bombay, June 18, 1947.

Kashmir was an independent sovereign state. As such, it was obviously contrary to international law to invade such a neighboring state. After having given an assurance that there would be no interference in the internal affairs of a state, after having categorically stated that such matters are primarily to be resolved between the ruler and the people of the state, there could be no justification whatsoever for Pakistan to intervene in Kashmir. Pakistan had never questioned the right of the ruler to act on behalf of the people of his state. Otherwise, Pakistan could not have entered into a Standstill Agreement with the ruler of Kashmir. It was only when the ruler acceded to India that Pakistan questioned his right to do so even though Mr. Jinnah had earlier given the states full freedom to opt for either India or Pakistan.

When the United Nations Commission for India and Pakistan visited Karachi in July 1948, facts could no longer be suppressed and the same Foreign Minister Sir Mohammad Zafrullah Khan informed the Commission that three regular Pakistani brigades had been fighting in Kashmir territory since May 1948. The Commission must have been taken completely by surprise. The UNCIP, in its First Report (S/1100, Paragraph 127) had this to say:

> The statements of the Foreign Minister of Pakistan to the effect that Pakistani troops had entered the territory of the State of Jammu and later his reply to the Commission's questionnaire that all forces fighting on the Azad side were under the overall command and tactical direction of the Pakistan Army, confronted the Commission with an unforeseen and entirely new situation. . . .
>
> According to the Security Council Resolution of the 17th January, the Government of Pakistan was requested to inform immediately the Security Council of any material change in the situation. In a letter addressed to the Security Council, the Pakistan Government agreed to comply with

this request. The Government of Pakistan have, however, not informed the Security Council about the presence of Pakistan troops in the State of Jammu and Kashmir. Sir Mohammad Zafrullah Khan explained that since the Commission had been charged to deal with the problems related to the Indo-Pakistan question, his Government thought that the information should instead be given to it. But he had been unable to do this previously because of the delay in the Commission's arrival in the subcontinent.

The Foreign Minister then told the UNCIP that Pakistan troops had been in Kashmir since May 8, 1948, the reason being that if they had not gone there, India would have taken over the whole area under occupation of the raiders. Surely, Pakistan had no justification to go into a territory where it had no legal or constitutional rights. The views of the Commission on this point were made clear in Appendix I to the enclosure of the UNCIP Report (S/1100, Paragraph 4). The Commission stated:

> The Security Council Resolution of 21st April 1948 which sets forth the terms of reference of the Commission, was adopted with the cognizance of the presence of Indian troops in the State of Jammu and Kashmir. The presence of Pakistan troops in J & K, however, constitutes a material change in the situation inasmuch as the Security Council did not contemplate the presence of such troops in that State, nor was it apprised thereafter by the Government of Pakistan.

In other words, there had never been any secrecy about the presence of Indian troops in Kashmir. India was exercising both its right and its duty to protect the state which had acceded to it. The Commission could not be expected to abet or condone Pakistani action of sending troops and raiders into the State of Jammu and Kashmir—an action which was contrary to international law. It is this unlawful presence of Pakistan troops in Kashmir, where they had no locus standii, that the Commission had to take into consideration in formulating its resolution dated August 13, 1948. It is for this reason that the resolution stipulated as the first preliminary step that Pakistan should agree to withdraw its troops from that state because the presence of Pakistan troops in the territory of the State of Jammu and Kashmir constituted a material change in the situation—a change which had been effected by Pakistan without any knowledge of the Security Council. The first and foremost condition of the truce was therefore the withdrawal of Pakistan troops. Throughout this resolution, UNCIP had always kept in view the lawful presence of Indian troops in Kashmir in contrast to the unlawful presence of Pakistani military forces in the state. If one reads the resolution, it will be obvious that it proceeded on a clear recognition of the fact that the sovereignty of the State of Jammu and Kashmir was vested in India. People's memories are short. This basic fact seems now to have been forgotten with the efflux of time. It is also apparently forgotten that Pakistan had invaded the state. This is what Sir Owen Dixon, the UN Representative for India and Pakistan, had to say:

> Without going into the causes or reasons why it happened, which presumably formed part of the history of the subcontinent, I was prepared to adopt the view that when the frontier of the State of Jammu and Kashmir was crossed on, I believe 20 October 1947, by hostile elements, it was contrary to international law, and that when in May 1948, as I believe, units of the regular Pakistan forces moved into the territory of the State, that too was inconsistent with international law.

Once Pakistan was forced to admit to the Commission that regular Pakistani troops were fighting in Kashmir, our complaint against Pakistan had been more than proved. Pakistan's action was contrary to international law and it was clearly guilty of an act of aggression. If, for argument's sake, we accept the Pakistan statement that its troops had been dispatched to Kashmir only on or after May 8, 1948, Pakistan's action was even more inexcusable as it was not only contrary to international law but also in flagrant violation of the Security Council resolution of January 17, 1948, which it had accepted. This resolution called upon both parties to refrain from permitting any acts which might aggravate the situation and which required that any material change should be communicated to the Security Council. Dispatch of troops was certainly an act which was bound to aggravate the situation. It was also a material change in the situation that had been reported previously to the Security Council. Pakistan had then denied its presence in Kashmir. Having proved our case we would have been perfectly justified in pressing the Security Council to ask Pakistan to withdraw from Kashmir. We were, however, persuaded to accept the resolutions of August 13, 1948, and of January 5, 1949, for the sake of peace and harmonious relations with a close neighbor. Before accepting the resolutions, we had asked for certain clarifications and only when these clarifications were satisfactory we accepted these resolutions. For instance, we had emphasized "that if the Government of India were to accept the Commission's plebiscite proposals, no action could be taken in regard to them until Parts I and II of the Commission's resolution of 13th August had been fully implemented." Parts I and II of that resolution refer to cease-fire and the truce agreement. We had also made it clear that "in the event of Pakistan not accepting these proposals, or having accepted them, not implementing parts I and II of the resolution of 13th August, the Government of India's acceptance of them should not be regarded as in any way binding upon them." * The Commission accepted this position. This was clearly a conditional acceptance of the resolution. There was no secrecy about it and Pakistan was well aware of the fact that if Pakistan did not act up to these resolutions by first withdrawing its troops and tribesmen from Kashmir, its acceptance of those resolutions would not be binding on India in any way. Even the UNCIP resolution of January 5, 1949, laid down that "a plebiscite will be held when it shall be found by the Commission that the cease-fire and the truce agreement set forth in parts I and II of the Commission's resolution of 13th August, 1948, had been carried out." Parts I and II of the resolution of August 13, 1948, have not been implemented because of Pakistan's refusal to withdraw its troops from Kashmir. The conditions have not been satisfied and India cannot be regarded as being bound by these resolutions any longer.

The only commitments we accepted were those contained in the UNCIP resolutions of August 13, 1948, and January 5, 1949, conditional upon the prior withdrawal of the Pakistani forces and nationals, the large-scale disarming and disbanding of the Azad Kashmir forces, the restoration of the unity of the State of Jammu and Kashmir, the return of refugees and upon the restoration of law and order and of conditions of security. None of these conditions has been satisfied. What is more, every one of these conditions has been violated by Pakistan. Pakistan's duty to withdraw its forces was unconditional. All the subsequent talks about synchronization of the withdrawal of troops and about balanced forces and so on, were not contemplated by the Commission in its own resolutions, which proceeded on the recognition of the unlawful presence of Pakistani armed forces and nationals in Kashmir.

* Security Council official records, Supplement for January 1949, Annex 4, Aide-Mémoire 1.

Pakistan deliberately dragged on the negotiations by raising such issues in the hope that with the efflux of time the people would forget Pakistani aggression in Kashmir as also the atrocities committed by the Pakistani raiders. As years rolled by, outsiders did forget the Indian complaint against Pakistan and tried to equate their presence in Kashmir. India being the aggrieved party was not prepared to be treated in the same way as the aggressor. While, therefore, we were always ready to discuss all proposals presented to us, we refused to agree to make any further concessions as soon as we realized that these proposals were intended to effect a material change in the position taken by the UNCIP, in its resolutions of August 1948 and January 1949. We were a party to the proposal made by the Commission in these resolutions subject to some conditions. If a proposal is accepted but not implemented, it cannot stand forever. We had made many offers to Pakistan at different times but they were not accepted. The offer must be deemed to have terminated when it is not accepted. In regard to demilitarization proposals a number of concessions were offered by us provisionally in the course of discussions. Since they were not accepted, they can no longer be binding on us. It would be impossible to conduct negotiations if one cannot make conditional offers or discuss tentative plans without being bound by them for all time. At no time did India abandon its sovereignty over the State of Jammu and Kashmir and it has never agreed to any resolution which even by implication questioned this sovereignty. We have taken care to see that this basic position is not departed from. That is why we could not accept his proposal when Sir Owen Dixon departed from the mandate of the Security Council and tried to create a new situation. That was the stand taken by us in regard to proposals made by General MacNaughton and Dr. Graham. It is in defense of this sovereignty that India has had to come in conflict with the People's Republic of China in Northeast Kashmir. The criticism that India did not accept any of the proposals made since the resolutions of August 13, 1948, and January 5, 1949, is quite unfair and unjustified. We are naturally not prepared to make any further concessions or to basically modify these resolutions, particularly as the modifications proposed so far have been only in favor of Pakistan.

These are the salient features of the Kashmir case. The more critical view taken by the Americans on India's stand on Kashmir is based on a number of misconceptions. Most Americans have been unable to get rid of the popular belief that British India was partitioned between Hindus and Moslems on the theory that they constitute two different nations. In other words, they accept the so-called two-nation theory. The Moslem League in pre-partition India no doubt advanced this theory, but the Indian National Congress, and Indians in general, never accepted the validity of this two-nation theory. They agreed to the partition as there was no other way of attaining independence. Indians cannot understand how Americans, of all people, can believe in this two-nation theory based purely on religion. The U.S.A. has been the meeting place of peoples professing different faiths and of diverse racial origin. How can Americans believe in the medieval concept of a religious state? Yet they accept Pakistan's claim to Kashmir based mainly on the ground that the majority of Kashmir's population is Moslem. In their view, it should therefore go to Moslem Pakistan rather than to the predominantly Hindu India. This is an oversimplification of the problem and completely ignores the fact that Indians never accepted such an absurd theory of nationality being based solely on religion. Even if one believed in this theory, it was in fact impossible to divide India entirely on the basis of religion. All that actually happened was that certain contiguous areas in old British India, which had a Moslem majority, wanted to secede from the rest of India and to form a new State of Pakistan. This secession was agreed to as a measure of compromise. Even after partition and the initial mass migrations, the 1951 census figures show that India was still left with some 37 million Moslems and Pakistan with over 9 million non-Moslems. This fact alone shows that British India could not have been divided into a purely Hindu India and a purely Moslem Pakistan, even if one ignores some 30 million people in India professing other faiths. If partition had really been made on the basis of religion, it would have been natural for all Moslems to have gone to Pakistan and for all non-Moslems to have come to India. It is also not so well known to Americans that the partition that created Pakistan was confined to the region that constituted old British India. The British Government had made it quite clear that the decision about partition referred only to British India and that it had taken an entirely different decision in regard to the Indian states.

Americans point out that Indian protest against Junagarh's accession to Pakistan must have been on the basis that the population there was Hindu. This is not correct. India protested because accession of Junagarh to Pakistan would have contravened the principle of geographical contiguity which was one of the principal considerations for accession. One has only to look at the map and it will be seen that the Junagarh territory had no contiguity with the territories of Pakistan and was intermixed with the territories of many other states, which had already acceded to India. If Junagarh had acceded to Pakistan its enclaves, surrounded on all sides by Indian territory, could not have been administered without constant friction between India and Pakistan. It is also a fact that the large majority of the people of Junagarh were opposed to the ruler acceding to Pakistan. In the case of Kashmir the principle of geographical contiguity was fully satisfied. Even if one were to take into consideration the wishes of the people of Kashmir at the time of accession, there can be no doubt that the National Conference, the party representing the largest majority of the people of Kashmir, was clearly in favor of the state's accession to India. The importance of the principle of geographical contiguity was emphasized by Lord Mountbatten in his address to a special full meeting of the Chamber of Princes on July 25, 1947. He said that "the States are theoretically free to link their future with whichever Dominion they may care. But when I say that they are at liberty to link up with either of the Dominions, may I point out that there are certain geographical compulsions which cannot be evaded."

Indians also find it difficult to understand why Americans are reluctant to consider the legal aspects of the question and why they do not wish to make any difference between the unlawful presence of Pakistan in Kashmir and the right and obligation of India to defend a state which has lawfully acceded to it. The Cyprus case was under consideration by the Security Council soon after the Kashmir case had once again been considered in the Security Council in February 1964. Some people had seen a similarity between the two cases and had felt that this parallelism had thrown the UN and the U.S.A. into a difficult dilemma. Whatever may have been the validity of the Zurich and London agreements, after the admission of Cyprus as a sovereign member state of the United Nations, interference by Turkey or Britain, even though permissible under those treaties, would appear to contravene the provisions of Article 2 of the United Nations Charter, in so far as it restricts the sovereignty of Cyprus. Article 103 of the Charter lays down that "in the event of a conflict between the obligations of the members of the United Nations under the present Charter and their obligations under any other international agreement, their obligations under the present Charter shall prevail." Despite this clear provision of the Charter, despite the pleading of Cyprus that they were unequal treaties thrust on the people of Cyprus, the representative of the United States of America made the following statement with all solemnity and emphasis:

> The Treaty of Guarantee forms an integral part of the organic arrangements that created the Republic of Cyprus. In fact, it is a so-called basic Article of the Constitution of Cyprus.

He continued:

> This Treaty or any international treaty cannot be abrogated, cannot be nullified, cannot be modified, either in fact or in effect by the Security Council of the United Nations. The Treaty can be abrogated or altered only by agreement of all the signatories themselves or in accordance with its terms.*

This is the categorical statement of the U.S. Representative, even though the treaties are undoubtedly in conflict with the United Nations Charter, and having regard to the provisions of Article 103 of the Charter, their validity is, to say the least, not entirely free from doubt. If these treaties were to remain valid and its sovereignty was to be so restricted it is doubtful if Cyprus was qualified for admission to the United Nations as a sovereign member state. The independence of India and Pakistan came not through a treaty, but by an Act of British Parliament—the Indian Independence Act of 1947, enacted on the basis of an agreement arrived at between the British Government and the leaders of what were to become free

---

* Security Council document S/PV.1096.

India and Pakistan. This Act has the same effect and force as an international treaty, as it came about through an agreement among three member states of the United Nations. The provisions of this Act are the very basis of independence of India and Pakistan, and cannot have any the less sanctity than the provisions of a treaty bringing about independence to a country. The Indian Independence Act of 1947 is at least not in conflict with any provisions of the Charter of the UN. At any rate, the provisions of this Act cannot certainly be questioned by the parties thereto, namely the United Kingdom, India and Pakistan.

Yet, contrary to the opinions expressed in the Cyprus case, the American member of the Security Council appears to have chosen to ignore the legal effects of the Instrument of Accession signed by the ruler of Kashmir. This accession was made in accordance with the Indian Independence Act of 1947, an Act of the British Parliament, which created India and Pakistan, read with another Act of British Parliament, the Government of India Act of 1935. These Acts do not provide for conditional accession, nor do they require that the will of the people must be ascertained before the accession can be final. Indians cannot understand why so much importance should be attached to the rights of the British or the Turks in Cyprus and the legal rights of India in Kashmir as a constituent state of the Indian Union should not be recognized at all. If the U.S. Representative is correct in what he stated in the Cyprus case he should admit that the Indian Independence Act must be accepted as it is, that the Security Council has no authority to abrogate, to nullify or modify it and that it can be altered only by negotiation or agreement of all the parties, or in accordance with its terms. As is well known, there has never been any question of modifying the provisions of the Indian Independence Act in any way, by agreement between the parties concerned, viz., the United Kingdom, India and Pakistan.

Americans sometimes plead that they have not really gone carefully into legal implications of the accession of the state since the British who are parties to the Indian Independence Act have not given much importance to this aspect of the question. It is unfortunately true that as late as February 1964 the Representative of the United Kingdom said in the Security Council:

> We consider it unrealistic to consider the status of Jammu and Kashmir purely in terms of the legal effect of the Maharaja's Instrument of Accession.*

The ruler's authority to accede was absolute under the Indian Independence Act of 1947, read with the Government of India Act, 1935. The British Government was the principal architect of these Acts. If in its wisdom that government did not think it necessary to provide for the ratification of the accession of the ruler by the people of the state, the Representative of the United Kingdom in the Security Council should be the last person who can be permitted to challenge the validity of the Acts of his own Parliament—Acts which received the assent of his own sovereign. British action cannot however be an excuse for the United States not to examine the legal aspects of the case. The British Representative himself expressed different views on the importance of treaties only a few days later when he said in the Security Council:

> This Council has responsibility for preserving international peace but that must be exercised in a manner consistent with the treaties upon which the independence of Cyprus and the constitutional rights of the communities depend.**

* Security Council document S/PV-1090.
** Security Council document S/PV-1095.

If the provisions of these Acts of British Parliament and the procedures laid therein relating to accession of Indian princely states to India or Pakistan are to be questioned, doubts can be cast on the accession of 565 states to India and Pakistan. If the will of the people must be ascertained in all these cases, that would be tantamount to challenging the integrity of India—a position which the Government of India can never accept. For Pakistan, the position would be even worse. Not only would its integrity be challenged because of the lack of popular ratification of the accession of the states to Pakistan, but also its very existence could be challenged, since unlike India, it had no separate identity until its creation by the Indian Independence Act of 1947. To question the validity of these Acts of British Parliament would thus have even more far-reaching consequences for Pakistan.

The argument that the status of Kashmir should not be decided in terms of legal arguments alone has of course some force, but then the Indian case does not depend only on legal arguments. We recognize that the Security Council is not and never was intended to be an organ like a court of justice, adjudicating on legal points. It is a political body and has to consider problems more from the political angle. At the same time, it cannot brush aside the legal arguments as if they were of no value. It was Grotius who said: "Most true is the saying that all things are uncertain, the moment man departs from law." The very purposes of the United Nations, as laid down in Article 1 of the Charter, are:

> to bring about by peaceful means, and in conformity with the principles of justice and international law, adjustment or settlement of international disputes or situations which might lead to a breach of the peace. . . .

Unless the Security Council takes into account the fact that
one party has valid legal claims, while the other party is in
unlawful occupation, how can it hope to bring about a settlement in conformity with the principles of justice and international law? It is for this reason that the legal position of the
parties has been so often emphasized. The political considerations arising in the Kashmir case are of course equally important and they have been equally emphasized by India.

The settlement of the Kashmir question on the basis that
Pakistan wants—and Americans seem to support—would be
a triumph for the Pakistani concept of a religious state as
against the Indian concept of a secular state. If Kashmir has
to be separated from India on the ground that the majority
of the people there profess Islam, this would be death to the
concept of a secular state. The Government of India would
then be under even greater pressure than in the past to convert India into a Hindu state like the Islamic state of Pakistan.
With a population of fifty million Moslems and thirty more
millions of Sikhs, Christians, Buddhists, Jains, Parsis and
Jews—this is something which India cannot possibly accept.
This would mean the disintegration of India. It would be
difficult to convince Indians that a religious state in India
was a bad thing while a religious state in Pakistan was good.
Pakistan has been doing everything possible to prevent the
secular concept taking roots even in India. As a religious
state, it has no use for its non-Moslem citizens whom it would
like to get rid of. The Pakistan policy of persecution of its
non-Moslem population has several objectives. First, by driving out minority communities, it succeeds in making the state
one hundred percent Moslem. Secondly, if the nine million
non-Moslems residing mostly in East Pakistan, the population
of which at present exceeds that of West Pakistan by approximately the same number, could be driven out, the population

of East Pakistan would be very nearly equal to the population of West Pakistan. The demand of East Pakistan for higher representation in the legislatures and in the services on the basis of its population would then lose its force. Thirdly, by driving the minority communities into India, it spreads the communal virus in India itself. By keeping alive this communal feeling, Pakistan hopes to convince the fifty million Moslems of India that they can never be sure of being able to live in peace and harmony in India. If Pakistan's plan succeeds, the unity of India would most likely be broken up, as the minority communities are far too large in number. If we really wanted to develop a Hindu state, the problem of minorities should not have worried us—as indeed it does not worry Pakistan. We are, however, determined to keep India as a secular state where everyone will have the same rights and privileges without regard to his religion. With a religious state next door as an example, we have to strive hard to maintain our secular ideal. India has received generous aid and encouragement from the United States in its social and economic development. But on the even more important problem of our national integration—the promotion of the idea of secularism, nondiscrimination between religions—we have not received any political or moral support. On the contrary, by espousing Pakistan's claim to Kashmir mainly on the ground of religion, Americans have, perhaps unwittingly, been supporting the pernicious two-nation theory. It is difficult for Indians to understand how the United States can be oblivious of the fact that by their policies and their attitude on Indo-Pakistan issues, they encourage the conception of a religious state and thereby endanger the very survival of India and the stability of the entire subcontinent. Economic aid, even aid on our border defense, would have no meaning if we were to be politically disintegrated. At a time when the United Nations

Organization is advocating the setting up of multiracial states in Africa, how can one support the concept of a nationality based entirely on religion?

There is one other factor which also deserves to be remembered and kept in view. For the Moslem community in India, already weakened by the partition in 1947, it would be disastrous if it were to be further weakened by an annulment of Kashmir's accession to India. For them it is a vital matter not to have their population reduced any further. Moslems are in a minority in every state of India, except Kashmir. It gives them some additional confidence to think that there is at least one state in India where they are in the majority. The accession of Kashmir to India was thus of considerable significance to them. The continuation of India as a secular state is of much greater importance for the minorities than for the majority community. A plebiscite or a referendum conducted on the basis of religion is bound to arouse communal passions once again. It may serve the short-term interest of Pakistan to drive out non-Moslems from East Pakistan to create a feeling of instability in India but in the long run Pakistan would suffer no less. Mass migration in millions as happened between 1947 and 1949 will, apart from causing untold human misery, ruin the economy of both countries. India certainly is not prepared to re-enact the horrors of partition which were witnessed at our birth as a free nation. These are some of the political considerations we have to keep in mind.

Mr. Gunnar Jarring of Sweden in his report to the Security Council dated April 29, 1957, did recognize this danger when he said that "on exploring this question of a plebiscite, I was aware of the grave problems that might arise in connection with and as a result of plebiscite." It is unfortunate for us that Americans take no notice of such a danger although *The New York Times* seems to reject the plea of self-determina-

tion for the Greek majority of Cyprus on similar considerations. In an editorial on February 19, 1964, it said:

> The Greeks must recognize that self-determination is not an
> absolute right when it imperils peace and that the prohibi-
> tion of *Enosis* has the same standing in international law as
> the prohibition of Austrian *Anschluss* to Germany.

Judging by the statements of the American Representative
in the Security Council, the editorial seems also to reflect the
views of the U. S. Government. Yet Americans still talk of
self-determination for Kashmiri Moslems despite the fact that
it imperils the peace of the entire Indian subcontinent and
the well-being of more than 550 million people.

Americans urge that Pakistan's claim to Kashmir does not
rest entirely on the argument that Kashmir has a majority of
Moslem population. In the American view, all that Pakistan
wants is that the people of Kashmir should be given the right
of self-determination. Indians would like Americans to pause
and reflect why, if Pakistan is so solicitous about the right of
Kashmiris to self-determination, did it in the first place have
to put economic pressure on Kashmir by cutting off essential
supplies even after signing a Standstill Agreement? When
that failed, why was this followed by an armed invasion, first
by the tribal people from Pakistan, and then by units of the
regular Pakistan Army? There was no talk then of self-determination. Even Hitler invoked the principle of self-determination for the Sudeten Germans *before* invading Czechoslo-
vakia. Pakistan chose to attack first and, when the attack
failed, invoked this principle. How can anyone take Pakistan's
solicitude for self-determination for Kashmiris seriously when
in a number of statements, President Ayub Khan himself has
made it clear that Kashmir is vital for Pakistan, not only politically but militarily as well. President Ayub Khan declared

at Dacca on October 18, 1961,* that "Kashmir was a life and death question for Pakistan, and without a solution of this problem, we cannot be assured of the safety of our territory, especially the Western Wing of our country." On July 19, 1961, President Ayub Khan said: "Kashmir is vital for us for fiscal as well as economic security." ** The issue, thus, is not the right of the people of Kashmir freely to express their wish, but that Kashmir is necessary to Pakistan for political and economic reasons.

The Charter of the United Nations, both in Article 1, Paragraph 2, and in Article 55, lays down that friendly relations among nations should be "based on respect for the principle of equal rights and self-determination of peoples." The language used refers to the principle and does not confer any right to any racial or religious group in a particular country to claim independence. Discussions in San Francisco indicate that the concept of self-determination was considered by the framers of the Charter, in relation to the aspirations of peoples who had not already attained a full measure of self-government. The principle implies the right of peoples to self-government but not the right of secession. Self-determination is an excellent principle, but it ought to be applied to those countries where by force of arms, by the vicissitudes of history, people are held under an alien rule. It is not, however, applicable to sections of a people. If the policy of self-determination were to apply to parts of constitutionally created states, most of them would be broken up. There are many states where there are different ethnic or religious groups, some of whom may have even started separatist movements. The plea of self-determination in a plural society would arouse racial or religious passions and could mean

* Pakistan *Times* of October 19, 1961.
** Ibid., July 20, 1961.

disruption and lead only to chaos. Most of the new states in Asia and Africa fall into this category. The Sudan is peopled by Arabs and Negroes. Somalis are spread over Kenya, Ethiopia and Somalia. Mali has a nomadic Tuareg population. Arab Algeria and Morocco have their Berber populations. Uganda and Nigeria have important minorities. If religious differences are to be the criterion for self-determination, few African states would remain united, as they have a Moslem population as well as a Christian or a pagan population. The province of Katanga in the Congo (Leopoldville) went to the extent of actual fighting to secure a separate independent existence. The United Nations had to work hard to prevent the secession of Katanga on the plea of self-determination. There are similarly different ethnic or religious groups in many Asian countries where demands for self-determination have been heard. Kurds in the Middle East, Karens in Burma, separatist movements in Indonesia, are but a few important examples. Even the older states with European population would not be safe. Must the United Kingdom allow self-determination to Wales and Scotland, France to Brittany, the United States to some of the Southern states, Canada to the French community, or Belgium to the Walloons? Numerous other cases could be cited. If religion is to be the sole criterion for self-determination, are we to separate Catholics from Protestants in Europe and America, or Moslems from Christians in the Near East or in Africa? Self-determination cannot be merely a process of disintegration or fragmentation. When self-determination is applied to minorities in a national state, often new minorities are created. That is what happened when Pakistan came into being through the partition of British India. Prime Minister Suhrawardy of Pakistan however declared in 1956 that despite the presence of nine million non-Moslems in the country, the creation of Pakistan had put an end to the two-nation theory on the basis of which Pakistan was created. "All of us," he said, "Moslems and non-Moslems, are Pakistanis first and last. . . . Once Pakistan was created, the two-nation theory lost its force, even for Moslems." * After the creation of Pakistan, it was no longer necessary to believe in the two-nation theory and he made it clear that self-determination is not the right of a new minority, even if it is nine million strong.

The membership of the United Nations since its creation has more than doubled itself. With rare exceptions, transfer of power from the colonial rulers to the people of the country was always made without a plebiscite or referendum. Independence was achieved through negotiations, and by arrangement with the principal political parties. Even the creation of Pakistan itself was not sanctified by an all-India plebiscite or a referendum. If such a plebiscite had taken place, the Moslems who remained in India would have voted against partition and it is doubtful if there would have been a majority of Moslem votes in favor of the creation of Pakistan. Only in one province, the North-West Frontier Province, and in one small district in the east—Sylhet—was a referendum made for special reasons. In the N.W.F.P. the party then in power happened to belong to the Indian National Congress, and was opposed to the Moslem League, which was demanding the creation of Pakistan. They boycotted the referendum as they were offered only the alternatives either of remaining with India or of joining Pakistan, but were not given the option of a separate independent existence. As a result of the boycott, half the electorate did not participate in the referendum; the majority of the remaining half, however, voted for Pakistan. The inhabitants of this area are still clamoring for

* The Economist, London, November 3, 1956, page 432.

an independent Pakhtoonistan. Pakistan has never conceded to them the right of self-determination. Sylhet, on the other hand, was only one district with a Moslem majority, in the then British Indian Province of Assam, which had a predominantly non-Moslem population. Its future could not be decided by taking the votes of the few members in the Assam legislature elected from Sylhet. The only satisfactory way of ascertaining the wishes of the people, in the circumstances, was by a direct referendum.

Apart from these two special cases, no plebiscite was held to determine whether the people of the subcontinent of India wanted freedom, or whether the majority of the Moslems living in the entire country wanted a partition. The British Government was satisfied that the Indian National Congress and the Moslem League, representing the people of India, wanted freedom and that the Moslem League, representing a large section of the Moslems, wanted partition. It therefore came to the conclusion that independence should be given and the country should be partitioned. In Jammu and Kashmir, the National Conference, as the party representing the overwhelming majority of the people of that state, fully supported and asked for the accession of Jammu and Kashmir to India. Through a Constituent Assembly of elected representatives, in which the representatives from the State of Jammu and Kashmir also participated, the Indian people gave to themselves a constitution of their own. General elections based on universal adult suffrage have taken place three times in all parts of India including Jammu and Kashmir. The people have already exercised the right of self-determination.

Self-determination is a democratic process. There is no universal adult franchise in Pakistan. There has not been a single general election to the National Assembly of Pakistan since its creation in 1947, not even on the comparatively limited franchise which was obtaining in the last days of the British rule. The President of Pakistan has repeatedly said that the people of Pakistan are not fit for a parliamentary system of government based on adult franchise. That is why, after 18 years of independence, the people of Pakistan are now being educated on the virtues of a system of basic democracy under which eighty thousand basic democrats elect members of the Provincial and Central legislatures on behalf of one hundred million Pakistanis! It is somewhat ironical that Pakistan should press for the democratic right of self-determination of the Kashmiris when its own citizens are not yet considered fit to elect their representatives through a direct election. Pakistanis are said to have forgotten the democratic self-expression which they had learned in British days. Civil liberties and universal adult franchise still elude the people of Pakistan, and it is difficult to take Pakistan's solicitude for self-determination seriously. It is indeed strange that a government that says that democracy is not suited to the genius of its own people should demand self-determination for the people of a neighboring country which has had elections on universal adult franchise three times since its independence. It is difficult to justify placing these same people under a basic democracy of the Pakistani variety on the plea of self-determination. Like the people of Pakistan, the people of Kashmir would then be denied the benefit of Article 21, Paragraph (3) of the Universal Declaration of Human Rights, which they enjoy at present. That Article lays down that "the will of the people shall be the basis of the authority of government; this will shall be expressed in periodic and genuine elections which shall be by universal and equal suffrage and shall be held by secret vote or by equivalent free voting procedures."

The question, however, is asked as to how the ruler alone

could decide the fate of three million people of Kashmir. One may put a counterquestion as to how other rulers could decide the fate of even larger number of peoples inhabiting their states. The princely states which acceded to Pakistan were not given any opportunity to exercise the right of self-determination, after the ruler had acceded to Pakistan. On the contrary, it was disclosed in the West Pakistan High Court, a few years ago, that the accession of Bahawalpur had been forced on the ruler of that state. The Khan of Kalat revolted against accession and was arrested and detained in 1958. In neither case was the principle of self-determination followed. Pakistan even purchased the territory of Gwadur from the Sultan of Muscat without giving any opportunity to its people to say whether in this the second half of the twentieth century they wished to be bought like chattel. British India itself was partitioned by the British Government after consultation with half a dozen representatives of the Indian National Congress and the Moslem League. Partitions of Bengal and the Punjab were decided by a small majority of members of the Legislative Assemblies of those provinces, who had been elected on a limited franchise. In Bengal the provincial Legislative Assembly decided by 126 votes to 90 that the Moslem majority areas should join Pakistan. This small majority decided the fate of 66 million Bengalis. The Punjab Legislative Assembly similarly decided the fate of 31 million Punjabis by a majority of 91 votes to 77. Are we to reopen all these cases in order to give the people an opportunity to express their views? The answer must clearly be in the negative. Right or wrong, these were the arrangements that were made in the Indian Independence Act of 1947 by the British Government in consultation with Indian leaders. If the validity of this Act is challenged on the ground that these arrangements ignored the principle of self-determination, the very existence of Pakistan can be challenged, since the people of British India—even the entire Moslem population—were never given an opportunity to speak for or against the creation of Pakistan. Who can say what the result of such a referendum would have been?

It may well be asked why despite this well-established principle and precedent, did we at all agree to consider the possibility of a plebiscite or a referendum? It is often urged that once we agreed to accept the UNCIP resolution of August 13, 1948, and January 5, 1949, we must now implement the proposals contained therein. The American attitude seems to be that no matter what happened in the beginning, no matter how unjustified Pakistan's presence in Kashmir might have been, once India agreed to accept these UNCIP resolutions, the past should be forgotten, since these events happened prior to these resolutions. The Representative of the United States in the 1091st meeting of the Security Council held on February 14, 1964, dismissed the origin of the dispute as being "complicated and deeply buried in the history of the great subcontinent" of India. He wants to start only from the UNCIP resolutions of 1948 and 1949 and refuses to look further back. It is unfortunate that he did not wish to look into the genesis of the case, for if he did, he would have remembered the basic complaint, which was aggression by Pakistan in Kashmir. He might also have appreciated the context in which India had accepted the resolutions. Even though the accession of Kashmir was legally and constitutionally final and complete, we accepted the UNCIP resolutions of August 13, 1948, and January 5, 1949, for the sake of a peaceful settlement. We had however made it clear that our acceptance was on the specific condition that if Pakistan did not act up to those resolutions by implementing Parts I and II of the Resolution of August 13, 1948, the Government of

India's acceptance of those resolutions would not be binding on them in any way. It had also been made clear that "the Pakistan forces must be withdrawn from the State before the Government of India could consider any further steps." * Despite this clear reservation on our part which was no secret, and was fully known to Pakistan, it chose not to comply with these resolutions. Pakistan should have known that non-implementation of the resolutions by it would make them inoperative and would terminate the offer implied therein. If Pakistan still decided to take the risk, it can blame no one but itself. We had then hoped that the conditions on the basis of which we had accepted these resolutions would soon be satisfied and that the plebiscite, if any, would be over in a few months' time. If the conditions had been faithfully observed, i.e., if all Pakistani troops and tribal raiders had been withdrawn, if law and order had been restored in the state, there would have been something to be said for the referendum in the interest of establishing harmonious relationship with a neighbor. It has to be remembered that in 1948 and 1949, we were still passing through the horrors of partition attended by communal riots and mass migrations in millions. Conditions in India and Pakistan at that time were, in any case, unsettled. The situation was still disturbed. A plebiscite in Kashmir then, involving the rousing of communal passions, in those circumstances could not have led to a very great worsening of the situation.

A few extracts from the statement made by Mr. Urrutia of Colombia in the 768th meeting of the Security Council held on February 15, 1957, would explain the circumstances in which India had accepted the UNCIP resolutions. Mr. Urrutia started by explaining that he had undertaken a special

---

* Security Council official records, Supplement for January, 1949, Annexure 4, Aide-Mémoire 2.

study of the voluminous records of the Commission because
the Chairman of the UNCIP during the discussions happened
to be the Representative of Colombia. This is what Mr.
Urrutia had to say:

> First of all, that when the Commission was asked whether it
> wanted to enter into a discussion on the legality of India's
> sovereignty over Kashmir, the Commission said, it would pre-
> fer not to do so; second, that when Mr. Nehru asked Mr.
> Lozano, whether the offer to hold a plebiscite would, in the
> Commission's view, entail an unconditional commitment, if
> the first and second parts of the Resolution of August 1948
> were not carried out, Mr. Lozano replied very definitely
> 'No.' It is very clear that there would be no commitment on
> India's part until after the first and second parts of the
> August Resolution have been complied with.

Mr. Urrutia then went on to say that:

> The Commission had provided for an arrangement, system
> or procedure that was to be carried out in six weeks or three
> months at the most. Advantage should have been taken of the
> favorable atmosphere of the climate that had been brought
> about in India: Mr. Nehru's acceptance and the confidence
> with which the Commission had inspired him to accomplish
> all this in three months.

These were the assurances and expectations under which,
in the words of Mr. Urrutia, "a compromise solution" was
arrived at "whereby it was possible to elicit an offer from
India to submit the final disposition of Kashmir to a plebiscite." The words "elicit an offer from India" are significant,
and indicate the confidence which the Commission had inspired in Mr. Nehru. In retrospect, it appears that such confidence was entirely misplaced. We are now asked to forget
all these assurances and implement the resolution not within

an outside limit of three months' time, but 18 years later, as if the resolution had come out of a vacuum, as if time had stood still all these years. The Representative of the U.S.A. on the Security Council is now unwilling to take the trouble to examine how this compromise solution was arrived at— under what circumstances and with what expectations. Having decided to ignore the facts of the case prior to the acceptance of UNCIP resolutions, Americans are now prepared to concede Pakistan's demand for being treated on an equal footing with India in Kashmir. They find India's attitude unreasonable when it refuses to be equated with Pakistan which has occupied two-fifths of Kashmir by force, in clear violation of international law. To allow this occupation to continue is wrong enough. To grant Pakistan any further concessions is to aggravate the wrong and is, therefore, naturally unacceptable to India. Any impression that India has been intransigent because it has rejected this or that proposal subsequently, would not be justified if it is remembered that India had already made the maximum concession when it agreed to accept the UNCIP resolutions of August 1948 and January 1949.

Eighteen years have elapsed since the resolutions were accepted. Pakistan deliberately chose not to comply with those resolutions in the hope that the fact of aggression would be forgotten with the efflux of time. There have been many changes in the Kashmir situation during these years. With all these changes, it is no longer possible to be bound by, or proceed on the basis of, those resolutions. We are not prepared to rouse communal passions and to have once again mass migrations and large-scale killings, which would spell the ruin of all that India has striven for and accomplished during the last 18 years.

How has the situation changed? The UN Commission itself stated in its report as follows: *

> There is indeed no doubt that the Azad forces now have a strength which changes the military situation, and to that extent, makes the withdrawal of forces, particularly those of India, a far more difficult matter to arrange within a structure which consists only of the regular forces of the two Armies. Although it might be a matter of discussion whether the numerical strength of the Azad Kashmir forces has actually increased since August 1948, there is no question that these forces who have since then been working in cooperation with the Pakistan regular Army and who have been trained and officered by that Army, have increased their fighting strength. It is reasonable to suppose that if the Commission had been able to foresee that the cease-fire period would be prolonged throughout the greater part of 1949 and that Pakistan would use that period to consolidate its position in the Azad territory, the Commission would have dealt with this question in part II of the Resolution of the 13th August.

Since the Commission submitted its report in December 1949 many more material changes have taken place in the context of the situation obtaining in 1948 and 1949. These are some of the major violations of the UNCIP resolutions on the part of Pakistan. In the first place, Pakistan did not withdraw its troops, nor did it make any efforts to disband the tribal irregulars. On the contrary, and in defiance of the resolutions, Pakistan augmented its military potential by using its membership of military pacts, by training up the Azad Kashmir irregulars to the level or regular troops, by importing new and more up-to-date arms and by the building of airfields in the Pakistani-occupied areas, thereby creating bases for attack against India and endangering its security.

* Document S/1430, Paragraph 225 of UNCIP, Third Interim Report.

Thus instead of withdrawing, Pakistan has consolidated its illegal occupation of the territory which it was required to vacate. Secondly, the illegal integration of the northern areas is in violation of the Security Council resolution of January 17, 1948, restricting any material change. Thirdly, instead of permitting the territory evacuated by the Pakistan troops to be administered by local authorities under the surveillance of the Commission, Pakistan is directly administering through what it calls the Azad Kashmir Government, which according to the Commission was not to be recognized. Instead of appealing to the people to assist in creating and maintaining an atmosphere favorable to the promotion of further negotiations, Pakistan has all along encouraged cries of "Jehad" or holy war. It is also organizing and financing subversion and sabotage in the State of Jammu and Kashmir. Lastly, having no common border with the People's Republic of China, Pakistan has nevertheless negotiated Kashmir's borders with Sinkiang, making a substantial change in the areas of the territories of the State of Jammu and Kashmir without even having the courtesy to inform the Security Council. This action is clearly in defiance of the Security Council resolution of January 17, 1948, which requires intimation to the Security Council of any material changes in the situation.

It is not for nothing that Ambassador Jarring had said in his report to the Security Council, on April 29, 1957:

> The implementation of international agreements of an ad hoc character which had been achieved fairly speedily, may become progressively more difficult because the situation with which it was to cope has tended to change.

That is precisely what has happened. It is too late in the day for anyone to suggest that we get back to the situation prevailing in 1948–1949.

The situation has since been further complicated by the forcible occupation of some 14,500 square miles of Kashmir territory by the People's Republic of China. Because of the continuing threat from China, withdrawal of Indian armed forces from Kashmir has now become impracticable.

The Kashmir problem is not the only problem between India and Pakistan. Pakistanis say, and many Americans believe, that the solution of the Kashmir question would make Pakistan friendly to India. We have settled so many problems with Pakistan, including the complicated Canal Waters question, which at one stage was considered to be the main stumbling block to Indo-Pakistan amity. Even after the solution of that question, relations did not improve. If the Kashmir problem could be solved, other problems would be created. Americans seem to imagine that if only the Kashmir question were solved, Pakistan would become friendly with India and would have no need for a special friendship with the People's Republic of China. The Foreign Minister of Pakistan, Mr. Bhutto, however, clarified the position in the Pakistan National Assembly on November 26, 1962, when he gave the assurance that Pakistan would never join India in any action against Communist China even if the Kashmir issue was solved.* Selig Harrison, writing in the Washington *Post* on March 10, 1963, reported: "Bhutto (Foreign Minister of Pakistan) recalled his statement in the November National Assembly that friendship with China is an independent factor in Pakistan foreign policy and that 'even if the Kashmir issue is settled amicably, we will not join India against China.'" Pakistan has been talking of a confederation with other countries but such is their antipathy toward India that even the expression of a pious hope that someday in the future

* *The New York Times,* November 27, 1962.

there may be some sort of a loose confederation in the Indo-Pakistan subcontinent is looked upon with suspicion as an example of Indian imperialism. The United States should not be carried away by the Pakistan plea that the solution of the Kashmir question will make Pakistan friendly to India. The causes of conflict are too many and far too deep and unless they can be tackled and mutual suspicion eliminated, the relations between the two countries cannot be improved. India has always tried to be friendly with Pakistan but such efforts have to be mutual if they are to bear fruit.

MILITARY AID TO PAKISTAN

THE American attitude on Kashmir, from 1950 onward, appeared to Indians to be changing more and more in favor of Pakistan. This development was generally attributed in India to the gradual American disillusionment with the Indian foreign policy. Prime Minister Nehru's visit to the U.S.A. in the latter part of 1949 removed whatever little hope the United States might have had of bringing India to align itself with the U.S.A. in its fight against Communism. With the emergence of a Communist China, the need for finding dependable allies in the region, to contain Communism, had become urgent. Mr. Nehru however made it quite clear, both in his public speeches and in his private talks, that India had definitely decided to follow a policy of nonalignment. This was a disappointment to the United States, and Mr. Nehru was thereafter looked upon as somewhat anti-American. The idea of having Pakistan as a military ally appears to have occurred about that time. There was a power vacuum in the area caused by the withdrawal of the British from India. Since India would not agree, Pakistan was the obvious alternative to fill up this vacuum. Late in 1953, strong rumors originated from Pakistan indicating that the United States would soon be concluding a military aid agreement with Pakistan. These rumors—which were later found to be calculated leakages from Pakistani sources—aroused suspicion in India. Approaches made by India, through diplomatic channels, to the United States evoked no satisfactory reply. It is unfortunate that further diplomatic approaches were given up and instead of keeping the matter for secret diplomatic negotiations, public statements were made in India pointing out our objections to military assistance to Pakistan. In some speeches made in December 1953 and January 1954, Mr. Nehru pointed out that by the grant of military aid to Pakistan "the region of Cold War comes right up to our border," and that an increase in the military potential of the Pakistan army through U.S. aid would have repercussions not only in India but also in the entire Southeast Asia. Pakistan would then be outside the area of peace which countries in South and Southeast Asia were hoping for. While admitting that we have no right to interfere with what Pakistan, an independent country, chooses to do, Mr. Nehru pointed out that "it became a matter of concern to us when such arming is accompanied by the type of outlook exhibited in the utterances of Pakistani leaders so full of hatred." These public statements had naturally no effect in the United States except to arouse some justifiable annoyance at what was considered as an Indian attempt to influence American foreign policy. The American reaction was that if India did not want military aid to defend itself that was no doubt its own business, but it has no right to object to Pakistan securing such aid if it so desires for its own defense. In retrospect, it would appear that India fell in the obvious

Pakistani trap that had been set up to arouse open Indian protest by allowing a calculated leakage. The United States had already promised to extend military aid to Pakistan, and would in any case have had no alternative but to go on with the military aid program, particularly after the news had leaked out. We need not, however, have made public protests and thereby given the excuse that such protests had made it even more difficult for the United States to back out from its promise of granting military aid to Pakistan. The fact that the arms aid decision was taken in February 1954 would seem to indicate that the Indian opposition could not perhaps have had any bearing on the basic question of aid, though it was taken as an uncalled-for interference by India in American defense and foreign policy.

On February 24, 1954, President Eisenhower wrote to Prime Minister Nehru assuring him that the military assistance given to Pakistan was intended specifically for the purpose of strengthening its defense against possible Communist aggression, that it was in no way directed against India and that every care would be taken to prevent any diversion of the U.S. military aid for use against India. Undoubtedly, the American objective in granting military aid to Pakistan and in setting up SEATO, a few months later, was to secure the defense of Southeast Asia against Communist expansion. As Mr. Nehru said in the Indian Parliament, he had no doubt as to the sincerity and goodwill of President Eisenhower toward India. At the same time, it is equally true that Pakistanis never made any secret of the fact that they wanted to build up their military strength, not for defense against possible Communist aggression, but for use against India. The statements of responsible leaders of Pakistan made it quite clear from the beginning that they had joined the military pacts only because of India—because of their desire to speak from a position of strength. *The New York Times* of January 21, 1962, reported President Ayub strongly criticizing the United States for having questioned the use of American arms in fighting on the Afghan border in September 1961. "Do they expect us to put them in cotton wool?" he is reported to have asked.

Pakistan, of course, never cared to conceal the fact that the arms buildup was for use against India. Many Americans also thought that Pakistan wanted American arms for use against India. An American correspondent after a visit to Pakistan wrote as follows:

> The average Pakistani thinks very little about the Communist threat, if he thinks of it at all. His hostility is toward India rather than the Soviet Union. And he assumes that in the event of a showdown with India, the American military supplies will be drawn upon.*

From discussions in the Senate Foreign Relations Committee, it is clear that at least some members of the Senate were also aware of the real objective of Pakistan. If despite that fact, the American Administration continued to believe that Pakistan was building up its defense against Communism and arms aid flowed to Pakistan in that belief, it is perhaps not entirely unreasonable on the part of Indians to feel that the decision to grant military aid to Pakistan was taken at least partly with the object of teaching a lesson to neutralist India.

In a series of three articles published on August 10, August 24 and September 7, 1959, in the *New Republic,* Selig S. Harrison has narrated how and why the United States came to take the decision of granting military aid to Pakistan, and later to set up the South-East Asia Treaty Organization which Pakistan joined as a member. According to him, the United

---

* A. T. Steele in the New York *Herald Tribune,* June 7, 1956.

States was influenced to take up this policy by the opinion of certain prominent British officials that Pakistan should be groomed to fill the vacuum created by Britain's withdrawal from the subcontinent of India. Apart from the British influence, "the Knowland-wing Republican desire to get tough with Nehru" played an important role in shaping this policy. Selig Harrison concludes by saying that Vice-President Nixon "urged this alliance [with Pakistan] not for its purported defense value against Soviet aggression, but for the very reason Pakistan had sought the aid—as a counterforce to the confirmed neutralism of Jawaharlal Nehru's India." No wonder many Indians suspected as much. It is possible to argue that despite Pakistani statements to the contrary, the United States still believes that when called upon to do so, Pakistan would honor its commitments as an ally and as a member of SEATO, to assist the United States in its efforts to contain Communism. It may be recalled that it was at the instance of the United States that SEATO extended its protective umbrella to Laos, Cambodia and South Vietnam, even though these countries were not members of SEATO. In the summer of 1962, when there was a feeling that the Pathet Lao might sweep down to the borders of Thailand, an American force of 5,000 to 6,000 troops was brought to Thailand with the concurrence of the Thai Government, in order to boost the morale of the people in the Southeast Asian region. Some other members of SEATO also sent token forces to Thailand on this occasion, but not Pakistan. When questioned, Pakistanis pleaded that Thailand had not asked for troops from Pakistan. In any case, Pakistan, according to them, was in no position to supply troops since it was afraid of possible attacks from India. India had then a whole brigade of troops in the Congo and was also contributing the largest contingent of troops to the UN Force in Gaza. Even so, Pakistan could not send even a token force to Thailand. Yet, the fear of attack from India did not prevent Pakistan from sending, within a few months, some 1,500 troops to West New Guinea, to constitute the UN Force there.

The real reason of course was not fear of India, but deference to the wishes of China. While obtaining large-scale military aid from the United States and joining the military alliances of SEATO and CENTO, Pakistan had at the same time given an assurance to China that the building up of its military strength would in no way ever be directed against Communist China. When the occasion arose for the first time, since the creation of SEATO, to demonstrate the determination to contain Communism, Pakistan backed out from its commitments without any apology. It was in a dilemma and was apparently more anxious to honor its secret assurances to China. It is for the same reason that in the SEATO meeting held in London in the beginning of May 1965, Pakistan refused to support U.S. action in South Vietnam. Pakistan of course cannot explain the real difficulty but Premier Chou En-lai gave out the facts in reply to a question put to him by the correspondent of the Associated Press of Pakistan in the course of an interview. The question was:

> How do you look at the Sino-Pakistan relations in view of the suggestions made in the press abroad that the Sino-Pakistan friendship is contradictory to Pakistan's membership of the SEATO and because Pakistan receives aid from the United States?

This is what Premier Chou En-lai said:

> "We do not deny that there is a certain contradiction. It is precisely for this reason that development of friendly relations between China and Pakistan has been a process of gradual accumulation. Shortly after the founding of new

China, China and Pakistan established relations of mutual recognition. Later, through the Pakistan Ambassador to China, a preliminary understanding was established between us. At the Bandung Conference, the Prime Ministers of the two countries met, and later they exchanged visits. The mutual understanding between our two countries was thus further enhanced. After the formation of SEATO in 1954 the Pakistan Government often declared to the Chinese Government that its participation in that organization was not for the purpose of being hostile to China and would not prejudice Pakistan's friendship for China. Since Mohammed Ayub Khan assumed leadership of your country as your President, facts have further proved that Pakistan's policy toward China is one of friendship and not one of hostility.

"Not long ago, in the United Nations, Pakistan cast its vote in support of restoration of new China's rightful position in the United Nations and did not support the U.S. position of retaining the Chiang Kai-shek clique in the UN. The most striking proof is the conclusion of the Sino-Pakistan boundary agreement. In disregard of India's position and U.S. pressure, Pakistan resolutely took the initiative to sign the boundary agreement with China. Thus we have further understood that Pakistan is genuinely desirous of maintaining friendly and good neighborly relations with China. . . .

"The relations between the United States and India have undergone a great change since the SEATO Treaty was signed. After the Geneva Conference on the Indo-China question, India still made a show of peace and neutrality. At that time, the U.S. chose Pakistan, Thailand and other countries to form SEATO which parades as an anti-Communist and anti-China military alliance. But the facts in the past few years show that Pakistan has not acted in accordance with U.S. wishes. Pakistan wishes to be friendly and not hostile to China. On the other hand, India's so-called peace and neutrality are only a façade.*

* Extracts from Premier Chou En-lai's interview with the correspondent of the Associated Press of Pakistan published in *Dawn,* Karachi, April 11, 1963.

The *Observer,* London, commented on July 21, 1963, that "it is significant, however, that Chou En-lai had told a visiting Pakistan delegation recently that China would defend Pakistan throughout the world as Pakistan defended China in CENTO and SEATO."

With these facts now coming out in the open, Indians have got confirmation to their belief—if any confirmation was needed—that Pakistan had all along been building up its military strength not for defense against possible Communist attacks as the United States believed and asserted, but for use against India, and for strengthening its bargaining position vis-à-vis India. Indians find it somewhat difficult to believe that with so many American officials—civil and military—living in Pakistan, and having so many sources of information available to it, the American Administration could really have been so ignorant of Pakistan intentions. Indians therefore draw the conclusion that the United States has built up and is still helping Pakistan to build up its armed strength knowing full well that American arms were more likely to be used against India and possibly against Afghanistan but none against China. The general feeling among Americans, however, still is that Pakistan is genuinely anti-Communist and is a loyal ally of the U.S.A. If it is now moving into the arms of China, that is because of its fear of India. By giving some military aid to India in the wake of the Chinese invasion in 1962, the United States believes that it lost the friendship of Pakistan. If only India would accede to Pakistani demands in regard to Kashmir, Pakistan could yet be prevented from moving closer to China. Instead of showing any annoyance toward Pakistan for its pro-Chinese move, Americans are therefore more inclined to show their annoyance to India. They refuse to take any cognizance of the repeated assertions made by Pakistani leaders that even if the Kashmir dispute were settled to the satisfaction of Pakistan, under no circum-stances would Pakistan ever go against China. Americans still like to believe that once Kashmir is out of the way, Pakistan would join India in the defense of the subcontinent—a belief which Indians cannot share, in view of clear statements to the contrary by Pakistani leaders. The Indian reaction, on the other hand, is that if the United States is prepared to be blackmailed by Pakistan that is no doubt its own business, but the United States has no right to expect India to pay the price demanded by Pakistan.

Americans seem to believe that the only way of keeping Pakistan away from Communist China is to persuade India to satisfy Pakistan by making some territorial concessions. Many other countries also wish to prevent Pakistan being irretrievably lost to Communist China. They all want India to pay the price for retaining Pakistan on their side. Similar pressure was exerted on us in 1963 by some friendly non-aligned countries when they urged India to come to terms with Peking by surrendering Aksai Chin. It is proposals of this sort, to placate the aggressor, that put an intolerable strain on our relations with friendly countries. We realize that driving Pakistan into the arms of Communist China would not be in our interest either, but yielding to blackmail is not the best way to meet this threat. It will only whet the appetite of the blackmailer and his demands will go on in-creasing. The world yielded to many of Hitler's demands but realized too late that his demands were insatiable. One can resist the blackmailer only by challenging him to do his worst and forcing him to face the consequences.

If our friends go on pressing us to make territorial sacri-fices in the name of peace, we may, as Prime Minister Shastri has already said, be driven to desperation, and that may not ultimately serve the global interests of peace. If friends desert us, Indian public opinion may well veer around to accept the pro-Chinese Communists' advice to compromise with Peking by giving up Aksai Chin, particularly since Ladakh would, in any case, be indefensible if the Kashmir Valley should go. Our main access to Ladakh would then be cut off. It is also said that by surrendering Aksai Chin we would merely give up some barren territory for which we have little use. On the other hand, by surrendering the Kashmir Valley, we not only surrender a larger territory but we also yield on a cherished principle by accepting the pernicious theory of Pakistan that Hindus and Moslems are two separate nations. An acceptance of the two-nation theory would not only destroy our concept of a secular democracy but would also threaten our very existence as a nation. We gain nothing in return—not even the promise of Pakistani support against China. Instead of making all this sacrifice, why not have an accord with China? So runs the line of argument of the pro-Chinese Communists of India, ignoring, of course, the fact that it is not so easy to arrange a compromise with China with honor and self-respect. China believes that India is the greatest obstacle to its ambitions in Asia, offering as it does a rival way of life. India could also be a formidable competitor once it builds up its military and economic potential. What Peking wants New Delhi to accept is its power proximity—a demand which we have to resist unless we are prepared to subordinate our foreign policy to that of China at its behest. If, however, we are left with the only alternatives of surrendering territories either to Pakistan or to China, the choice may well be to attempt to buy a temporary peace by yielding to Peking. This is a possibility which cannot be completely ruled out. The situation might have been otherwise if peace with Pakistan had ensured a joint defense of the subcontinent against the People's Republic of China.

The continued flow of military aid to Pakistan, when there can no longer be any doubt as to the real objective of Paki-

stan, has only caused more concern to Indians. The first submarine was received by Pakistan as a gift from the United States on August 29, 1964. More supersonic planes are said to be on the way to strengthen the Pakistani Air Force. Against whom is a submarine needed? Surely, not against the Chinese, with whom Pakistanis have now built up cordial relations. Pressure is now mounting on the Indian Government to acquire a submarine from somewhere. Both the U.S.A. and the U.K. have shown great concern for Pakistan's objection to military aid to India. Pakistan's protests against military aid to India were received with great sympathy both in the U.S.A. and the U.K. No one reminded the Pakistanis of the much more massive military aid that they had been given over the last decade, by the U.S.A., with the avowed object of containing the Communist Chinese whom they are now befriending. According to American newspaper reports, the aid in military hardware alone till the beginning of 1963 is said to have been of the order of $1.3 billion. Thomas Brady, writing from Karachi, reported that Mr. Dean Rusk declared in Karachi on May 1, 1963, in the CENTO Council that U.S. aid to Pakistan up to date had been over three billion dollars. "The figure on military aid in the nine years since the alliance was formed has been kept secret at Pakistan's request." *
There is no way therefore of finding out the exact amount of military aid. Another figure quoted for the period ending fiscal year 1959 amounts to $981.7 million, of which military equipment was worth $536.7 million and the remaining $445 million had been given for defense support and direct forces support.** No figures are available for the period after 1959 though there is no reason to think that the aid has been on a

---

* *The New York Times,* May 2, 1963.
** *Defense of the Middle East,* by John C. Campbell (Praeger publications), 1960, pages 200–201.

lower scale thereafter. Yet the Pakistanis complain of the military assistance received by India from the U.S.A. in 1962–63 and 1963–64, totaling $165 million, half in credits and half in grants. There is a likelihood of similar assistance to the value of $400 million spread over the next four years. Indians find it difficult to understand why the United States should be so worried about Pakistani protests against comparatively much smaller military aid to India which had to defend itself against Communist China. India has given an undertaking not to use any part of the military aid received from the U.S.A. or U.K. against Pakistan. Pakistan never gave, nor was ever asked to give, any such undertaking. The least that the United States should have done was to ask for a similar undertaking from Pakistan not to use American weapons against India. In fact, Pakistan has always resented American assurances to India against any misuse of American military aid to Pakistan. The assurance given by President Eisenhower in 1954 proved quite illusory when American-supplied tanks, supersonic planes, air-to-air missiles and other sophisticated weapons were freely used by Pakistan in its undeclared war against India in April 1965 as well as in August and September 1965. In vain did India remind the American administration of these assurances. Many Indians could appreciate that the Americans were hardly in a position effectively to prevent the abuse of the weapons already given to Pakistan as military aid. What irritated them, however, were statements emanating from high American quarters to the effect that both India and Pakistan were using American weapons. This was not only another attempt to equate India and Pakistan but the statements were factually inaccurate. India did not use any American military aid against Pakistan. In fact, the type of military aid that was received by India would have been of little use in the fighting against Pakistan. While American military officers were given ample opportunities by India to satisfy themselves on this point, Pakistan refused to offer any such facilities to them.

The Communist Chinese ultimatum to India in September 1965 was well coordinated with Pakistan's activities, which did not go unnoticed. An article in the *New Statesman,* London, commented as follows:

> The virtual withdrawal of the Chinese ultimatum to India was timed so perfectly to coincide with the arrival in New York of the Pakistani Foreign Minister, that it is reasonable to suppose that it was the result of close diplomatic liaison between Rawalpindi and Peking.*

It is ironical that U.S. military aid to Pakistan which was intended to help in containing Communism should have been used against India. It would indeed be tragic if Pakistan, a SEATO ally of the U.S.A., were to use American arms against India, in concert with Communist China.

Americans are inclined to believe that Pakistan is really afraid of India. If that were really so, Pakistan should not have consistently refused India's offer of a no-war pact. Pakistan's security is guaranteed through military pacts such as SEATO and CENTO in which the United States, Great Britain and France—not to mention the other members of SEATO and CENTO—are committed to come to the assistance of Pakistan in the event of an attack from some other country. It has also got a separate military aid agreement with the U.S.A. Not content with these assurances from all the Western great powers, Pakistan has now obtained also the protection of the People's Republic of China. On July 17,

---

* "China and the Ceasefire," by Roderick MacFarquhar, *New Statesman,* London, September 24, 1965.

1963, initiating a foreign policy debate in the Pakistan National Assembly, the Foreign Minister, Mr. Bhutto said: "In the event of a war with India, Pakistan would not be alone. . . . Pakistan would be helped by the most powerful nation in Asia."

This was confirmed by the Chinese Vice-Minister of Foreign Trade, Nan Han Chen, during his visit to Pakistan in December 1963. He told his Pakistani audience: "If ever there is a war between India and Pakistan, China will surely support Pakistan."

Can anyone believe that Pakistan is really afraid of India—a country now threatened by the People's Republic of China which has the largest conventional army in the world estimated to be three million strong? On the contrary, it is because it knows very well that there is no risk of an attack from India that Pakistan can afford to spurn the offer of a no-war pact made by India.

It is sometimes asked how it is possible for a comparatively small country like Pakistan to provoke a larger country like India or to aggravate tensions. The answer to that query has perhaps been furnished in an article published in the January 1965 issue of *Foreign Affairs:*

> Pakistan has been able to acquire a disproportionately strong power position relative to that of India through alignment with the United States. As an ally permitting the use of its territory, for strategic intelligence purposes, Pakistan has commanded from the United States an economic and military aid subsidy much larger than her size would otherwise warrant. Rawalpindi has been emboldened by this to think big and press for Indian concessions from a position of artificially induced strength. . . .

> The special nature of the Pakistan link [with the U.S.A.] has been sharply underscored in the American refusal of In-

dian requests for supersonic aircraft, air-to-air missiles and heavy tanks, all of which has been given to Pakistan.*

Americans feel particularly hurt that their efforts to find a solution of the Kashmir problem are looked upon with suspicion in India. It is true that Indians do not think that Americans can be impartial on this issue. Whatever may have been the benefit that the United States may have got out of its military alliance with Pakistan, it is certain that this military alliance made it impossible for the United States to play any useful role thereafter in Indo-Pakistan disputes. Indians cannot perhaps be blamed too much if they find it difficult to believe that the United States can be impartial or objective in a dispute between a trusted ally like Pakistan and non-aligned India.

In *The New York Times* of September 6, 1964, Thomas J. Hamilton wrote:

> Soon after Stalin's death in 1953, the men in the Kremlin became aware of the political advantages to be gained from supporting neutralist Asian and African states against the Western powers and also against any newly independent state that sided with the West.
>
> Thus it is now a foregone conclusion that whenever the Security Council takes up the Palestine question, for example, the Soviet Union will veto any resolution unacceptable to the Arab nations. It is equally certain that a Soviet veto will prevent the Council from adopting any resolution on Kashmir that is opposed to by India.

It did not perhaps occur to Mr. Hamilton that a Russian may with equal logic say that soon after 1953, the United States became aware of the political advantages to be gained by supporting its allies against neutralist Asian and African

---

* "Troubled India and Her Neighbors," by Selig S. Harrison.

states. For, if it is true that the Soviet Union would be inclined to support India on the Kashmir question, it is equally true that the United States would be inclined to support Pakistan on the Kashmir question. Whether a Russian will say so or not, many Indians rightly or wrongly believe that India cannot expect any support from the United States against Pakistan, at any rate for the present.

GOA

INDIA's action in Goa in December 1961, putting an end to the last vestiges of colonialism on Indian soil, aroused great indignation and came in for outright condemnation in the entire Western world. Prime Minister Nehru himself had stated to press correspondents in New Delhi on December 18, 1961: "It was no pleasure to us to undertake armed action, but the Portuguese left no choice open to us." * India should have anticipated and was indeed prepared for a certain amount of criticism from West European powers who had colonies of their own. The virulence of the criticism that the action aroused in the United States of America, however, came as a surprise in India. Indians had hoped for some understanding of their action at least in the U.S.A. which itself had broken away from the colonial yoke through a war of independence. Instead, the Representative

* Reproduced from *India News* of January 1, 1962, issued by the Embassy of India, Washington.

of the U.S.A. in the Security Council made a more forceful condemnation of the Indian action than any member other than the Portuguese. The fact that the same action was supported and even applauded in the countries of Africa, Asia and Eastern Europe was contemptuously dismissed with the comment that these countries are guilty of setting up a "double standard." It never occurred to anyone even to try to understand their reasoning. All sympathy was with Portugal. One American newspaper calmly suggested that India should be driven out of Goa, which should be restored to the Portuguese. While deploring the Indian action, the Representative of the United Kingdom in the Security Council had said:

> "We do not underrate or discount in the least the strong feelings of many people in India at the continuance in the Indian subcontinent of these small areas still under foreign rule. ... We recognize that the Government of India has in the past made efforts to settle them by direct negotiations with the Government of Portugal." *

He had also quoted the words used by the Secretary of State for Commonwealth Relations in Parliament on the 18th of December:

> "We have long understood the natural desire of the Indian people to incorporate these territories in the Republic of India, and their feelings of impatience that the Portuguese Government has not felt disposed to follow the example of Britain and France. Nevertheless, I must make it plain that His Majesty's Government deeply deplore the decision of the Government of India to use military force to achieve its political objectives." **

* 987th meeting of the Security Council held on December 18, 1961.
** Ibid.

In the statement of the Representative of the United Kingdom there was at least a reference, however indirect, to Portuguese intransigence. There was not a word of this nature in the statement of the Representative of the United States. When the Security Council failed to take any action, he alone among all the members of the Security Council said that consultations regarding further steps which might be taken by the United Nations would continue and that he reserved his right to seek a further meeting at any time. If no further steps were in fact taken by the U.S.A., that was mainly because the Africans and most Asians made it clear that it would be unprofitable to take the matter to the General Assembly.

If one examines and analyzes the American criticism, it will appear that much of it arose from ignorance or misconception of facts. The gravamen of the charge was that India had committed an aggression against Portugal and had contravened the provisions of the Charter of the United Nations. "Geography is one very important factor in a nation's thinking. The world looks different from different parts of it. Problems look different and the importance of a particular problem also often appears to be different. Something small but nearby appears more important than something big but far away. The second important factor is the conditioning of the people, their past history, experience, etc., which make them think in a particular way or look at problems with different emphasis." * It is because of these differences in outlook that India's action in Goa came in for so much criticism in the Western world, while the same action received almost universal approval and support in African and most Asian countries. This is not due to any perversity on the part of Asians or

* Prime Minister Nehru's Press Conference at New Delhi on December 28, 1961.

Africans; nor is it fair to accuse them of having double standards.

Both geography and the conditioning of the people as also their recent history account for this difference of opinion and approach. To the American, Goa is a little distant place which is of no consequence. Many had perhaps never heard of Goa before this incident. Most people did not know that the inhabitants of Portuguese India were in no way different from the inhabitants of British India or French India. When I was speaking on Goa before a Canadian audience I was asked whether India would support American Indians if they were to claim that Canada should be returned to them and that Canadians should be asked to go back to Europe from where they had originally come. I could not at first understand the relevance of this question until I found that they were under the impression that the Portuguese had settled in Goa in the same way as the British and the French had settled in Canada. It was apparent that they were carried away by the Portuguese declaration that Goa is a Province of Portugal. A mere declaration by Portugal that Goans are Portuguese cannot of course change the facts of geography or of history. This declaration had, however, obviously created some confusion and misunderstanding in Canada and perhaps in the United States as well. Was Goa in Portugal? No; it was thousands of miles across the sea from Portugal. Were the people of Goa of Portuguese origin? No; the people are ethnically the same as those in the surrounding territories of India. Apart from Portuguese armed forces stationed in Goa, less than 1,400 civilians of Portuguese origin were living in 1961 in Goa, which had a population of 650,000. Most of the people of Portuguese origin were civil servants and businessmen temporarily residing in Goa. Even these few had not settled there; they still retained their domicile in metropolitan Portugal. The entire population of Goa is racially of Indian origin. The language of the people is the same as the language of the adjoining areas and not Portuguese. Very few people cared even to learn Portuguese. When a young Goan thought of learning a language other than his own mother tongue, more often he preferred to learn English rather than Portuguese, because English was much more useful. The manners and customs of Goans are exactly the same as those of other Indians. Goans are thus Indians by race, religion, language and culture. That is why Goans were always given all the rights and privileges of Indians even when they were still under Portuguese colonial rule. Not only were Goans employed in the civil services of India, many senior officers in our armed forces were also Goans. Some of these Goan officers actually took part in the military action against the Portuguese armed forces in Goa. The only Indian Cardinal, Cardinal Gracias, Archbishop of Bombay, is of Goan origin.

We never recognized the sovereignty of Portugal over Goa. Portugal occupied Goa by force. It was a clear case of aggression. It was the continuing Portuguese colonialism which constituted a permanent aggression and intrusion on the territories of India. To turn out an aggressor from one's territory cannot be called aggression. India's action could be regarded as aggression if Goa and the rest of India could be thought of as two separate countries. Goa and the rest of India are undoubtedly parts of the same country. One part of the country had become independent earlier than the other. The independence of India was not complete until the whole of India was freed from every vestige of colonialism on its soil. India could be charged with aggression if Goa had really been a part of metropolitan Portugal. The Portuguese claim that Goa is an integral part of Portugal was rejected by the General

Assembly in its Resolution 1542 (XV), when Goa and its dependencies were included as non-self-governing territories.

India has been criticized for having violated the provisions of the Charter. The Representative of the United States referred to the Preamble of the Charter which states that "the people of the United Nations are determined to save succeeding generations from the scourge of war," and "to practice tolerance and live together with one another as neighbors." He also referred to Article 2, Paragraph 4 of the Charter: "All members shall refrain in their international relations from the threat or use of force against the territorial integrity or political independence of any State, or in any other manner inconsistent with the purposes of the United Nations." * The U.S. Representative did not however refer to Paragraph 1 of Article 1, which says that "the purposes of the United Nations are: . . . to bring about by peaceful means, and *in conformity with the principles of justice and international law,* adjustment or settlement of international disputes, or situations which might lead to a breach of the peace." Nor did he refer to Paragraph 3 of Article 2, which says that "all members shall settle their international disputes by peaceful means and in such a manner that international peace and security, *and justice* are not endangered." He started off by saying, "I do not at this time propose to concern myself with the merits of the dispute." By refusing to consider the merits of the case, he avoided getting involved in the principles of justice, and that may be the reason why he did not refer to Paragraph 1 of Article 1, or Paragraph 3 of Article 2 of the Charter, both of which raise the question of justice. One cannot consider a case without going into its merits. No two cases can be exactly similar, and each case has

* 987th meeting of the Security Council held on December 18, 1961.

to be considered on its merits. If one had gone into the question of merits, the question of justice would have automatically come in for consideration. No solution, peaceful or otherwise, can be durable if it is not just. Lasting peace can never be realized so long as unjust conditions are allowed to prevail.

While India was criticized for having violated the provisions of the Charter which enjoin that all international disputes should be settled by peaceful means, the critics seemed to ignore the fact that this provision of the Charter is qualified by the words "in conformity with the principles of justice." These "principles of justice and international law," so far as they are applicable in the case of non-self-governing territories like Goa, are set forth in great detail in Article 73 of the Charter. This Article recognizes the "principle that the interests of the inhabitants of these territories are paramount" and requires the colonial powers "to transmit regularly to the Secretary-General" information regarding their colonies. Portugal consistently violated the provisions of Article 73. There was hardly any criticism in the West of this persistent violation of Article 73 of the Charter, or of the repeated disregard of the specific resolutions of the General Assembly bearing on this subject. While the Representative of the U.S. waxed eloquent on India's violation of the Charter, not a word was said by him about the Portuguese violation of the Charter or its flouting of the General Assembly resolutions.

One may ask why the continued violation of Article 73 of the Charter did not come in for any condemnation in the West. This can only be attributed to a difference in outlook. To the Western critic colonialism is bad, but not quite as reprehensible as it appears to the Asian and the African. To him continuation of colonialism and violation of Article 73

of the Charter were regrettable, but did not call for any condemnation. The Charter stands not only for peaceful methods, but also for the principles of justice. Yet, to our Western
critics, all that mattered was that the Charter's provision for
peaceful settlement of disputes had been violated. The fact
that the action was in conformity with the principles of justice, or that the Portuguese had been consistently violating
specific provisions of the Charter, was apparently of no consequence to them. To the Asian and the African, on the other
hand, because of their past conditioning, continuance of colonialism is intolerable, and the violation of Article 73 of the
Charter indefensible. Recourse to force was regretted, but was
not condemned since Portugal had barred the doors to all
attempts to settle the problem peacefully. In a conflict between "peaceful methods" and "principles of justice," the
latter was given greater importance. If a compromise had to
be made when these two principles came in conflict, they
would compromise rather with the principle of nonviolence
than with the perpetuation of Portugal's colonial rule, which
was the only alternative. Such compromise with principle is
of course unfortunate, but in mitigation one may point out
that this is not unknown in the West either. Western countries believe in democracy; anti-Communism is also an article
of faith with them. When these two principles come into conflict, they compromise with democracy rather than with anti-
Communism. By no stretch of imagination can some of the
countries allied to the West be considered to be democratic
or to be a part of the free world. An alliance with such countries can be justified only on the principle that they are, or at
least profess to be, anti-Communist. In a conflict, the principle of freedom and democracy is sacrificed. In fact, such
countries, merely because of their alliance with the West,
are considered part of the free world and are supported

against democracies, if they happen to be nonaligned. An East European delegate's quip was that Americans were so angry because India by its action had destroyed the only three remaining bits of the free world on Indian soil; Goa, Daman and Diu. Portugal of course belongs to the free world.

Even the nineteenth-century concept of sovereignty did not deny subject people their inalienable right to revolt against the colonial power. The whole of America, North and South, except Canada, was freed by violent revolutions, assisted by the French in the case of the U.S.A. and by the British in the case of certain South American countries. In those days sovereignty of the colonial power was recognized, but even so no one characterized these revolts as aggression against England or Spain. International law is not static, but is developing all the time. The present position is that sovereignty vests in the people. Article 73 of the Charter which deals with non-self-governing territories does not speak of sovereignty of the metropolitan power over its colonial territories, but refers to colonial powers as those "which have or assume responsibilities for the administration of territories whose people have not yet attained a full measure of self-government." They are also expected to "accept as a sacred trust the obligation to promote . . . the well-being of the inhabitants of these territories." In this view, we can no more speak of the sovereignty of an administering power over its non-self-governing territories than we can speak of a trustee's right to the property he holds in trust. No one can defend a trustee who misappropriates the property instead of returning it to the beneficiary.

Africans and Asians find it difficult to understand how the United Nations Charter framed in the middle of the twentieth century could possibly have taken away the inherent rights of the subject people to fight for their independence. If use of force is contrary to the Charter in all circumstances, irrespective of the merits of the case, subject people would have no redress against an intransigent colonial power which insists on the perpetuation of its rule. In that view, had the United Nations existed at the time, the American War of Independence would have been condemned, and British authority maintained. Similarly, Cavour, Mazzini and Garibaldi would also have been condemned for fighting against Austrian authority. The framers of the Charter were not, however, so unreasonable. They were realistic enough to understand that peace without justice could never bring about a stable solution of any dispute. When the Charter outlawed war, the object obviously was not to perpetuate the status quo of 1945. It is important to remember that the words "in conformity with the principles of justice and international law" in Paragraph 1 of Article 1, and the words "and justice" in Paragraph 3 of Article 2, were not included in the Dumbarton Oaks text, but were specially inserted at the San Francisco Conference. The memories of Munich were apparently still fresh and the framers of the Charter were fully conscious of the need to ensure justice while maintaining peace. They did not believe that peace could be maintained at the cost of justice. There was a clear recognition of the fact that peace without justice would be peace of the grave. Hence they made it an important qualification in the Charter itself by introducing the concept of justice and international law.

The Preamble of the Charter lays down as one of its objectives "to ensure, by the acceptance of principles and the institution of methods, that armed force shall not be used, save in the common interest." We have accepted the principles but have so far neglected to institute methods and devise means whereby changes can be brought about peacefully. Our Western critics laid all the emphasis on the provisions of the Charter enjoining peaceful settlement of disputes, but did not care to inquire what methods were available to persuade Portugal even to agree to discuss the matter. There could be no question of effecting a peaceful change when all talks were barred. Asians and Africans, on the other hand, while recognizing the importance of methods, placed greater emphasis on the ultimate objective, which is justice. It is true that the end cannot justify the means, but if no peaceful methods are open, violence cannot be completely ruled out, if that is the only way to bring about justice. The framers of the Charter certainly were not oblivious to the merits or to the justice of the case; nor did they insist on settlement of disputes by peaceful means irrespective of all other considerations. If peace must be maintained at all costs, irrespective of the considerations of justice, there can be no justification for the continuing Cold War. One party has only to accept the view of the other; there would then be no occasion for a conflict. The conflict does arise because the parties have different conceptions of justice. The attitude of the Africans and Asians reflects their own conditioning, viz., their uncompromising hostility toward colonialism. To them colonialism is unmitigated evil and is unjust. Here is a basic difference in thinking. The mental approach is different. Much can be said on either side, and one can argue the relative merits of the particular approach at great length. It is therefore important to remember that before condemning anyone, one should try to understand the logic of the other man's way of thinking.

The Representative of the United States had stated in the Security Council that India could not lawfully use force against Goa, especially when the peaceful methods in the Charter had not been exhausted. Let us examine the validity of this complaint. The whole of India was under European colonial domination. The British occupied the bulk of India, but they allowed certain small areas to be held by France and Portugal. These were not held with the consent of Indians, nor was such division of India between the colonial powers of Indians' own seeking. In 1947 the British agreed to leave India peacefully and there was an amicable transfer of power from British to Indian hands. The French took a little longer time, but they agreed to leave their colonial territories in India after some negotiation, again through peaceful means. We tried the same method with the Portuguese for fourteen years, but they just refused even to talk on the subject because they claimed Goa was an integral part of Portugal. Following the precedent of Gandhian nonviolent methods which had proved effective against the British Government in India, a few hundred volunteers went to Goa to demand independence. The Portuguese army shot to death twenty-two of these peaceful demonstrators and wounded another 225 of them. There was hardly any criticism of this brutality in the Western world. During all this long period of fourteen years, and even during the early part of December 1961, when the situation was taking a very serious turn, not one of Portugal's friends, who later condemned us for not continuing the negotiations, put any pressure on Portugal at least to discuss the question of Goa with us. Their sympathies were with little Portugal whom they wrongly considered to be the underdog, forgetting the atrocities that were being committed by it against the people of Goa.

Repression went on mounting. Civilian administration was withdrawn into Panjim leaving the bulk of Goa to the lawless elements and to the military. Public opinion in India was getting stronger and stronger in favor of some action and just at the psychological moment, the Portuguese for some strange reason aggravated the situation by firing on our passenger ships and our fishing boats, killing two people. There were also raids by the Portuguese into neighboring Indian territory. The Portuguese had apparently told some of their friends that it would be extremely embarrassing for them to leave Goa voluntarily through negotiations, since that would create a precedent for them to leave Angola and Mozambique also peacefully, through negotiations. If they had to leave, they would prefer to be ejected forcibly, since that would create less embarrassment for them vis-à-vis their other colonies. The Portuguese Government had made it clear that it would not allow transfer of sovereignty over Portuguese territories in the Indian peninsula to the Indian Union by peaceful means. Statements were also made openly and publicly by Dr. Salazar that he would adopt a scorched-earth policy—a policy which he had in fact proceeded to implement and would have completed, but for the Indian intervention. The Government of India moved in to prevent greater bloodshed. While it is most regrettable that force had to be used, it is well to remember that the total casualties in this operation were just a little higher than those caused by the Portuguese firing on unarmed volunteers in 1955. Incidentally, it showed the absurdity of the Portuguese claim that Goans are Portuguese. There was not only no resistance, but Indian soldiers were welcomed and received with jubilation by the local people.

The Secretary-General of the UN in his appeal of December 15, 1961, addressed to both parties, pleaded for negotiations in accordance with the principles of the Charter and the principles formulated by the United Nations. These principles are embodied in Resolutions 1514 (XV), 1542 (XV) and 1654 (XVI), on decolonization. The Portuguese in their reply dated December 16, 1964, refused to negotiate on this basis. They were prepared to talk only on the basis that Goa was an integral part of Portugal and they were prepared to negotiate for solution of the problems that might arise between the territories of the Portuguese state of India and those of the Indian Union—problems that might arise because of their close proximity. They thus wanted the negotiations only to secure an Indian confirmation of their absurd claim that Goa was an integral part of Portugal. In other words, they wanted Indian agreement to the perpetuation of their colonial rule over Goa. The answer to the question of the United States Representative as to why we did not negotiate further, was given by the Portuguese Representative himself. The utter futility of negotiations was made quite clear by him. The door to negotiation was completely barred. The Portuguese were violating the provisions of Article 73 of the Charter with impunity and they also flouted the General Assembly resolutions on the subject. Portugal thus rejected all peaceful methods of solving this question.

Fears have also been expressed that Indian action in Goa might perhaps be "the first act in a drama which could end with the death of the organization." It is difficult to understand why India's partial violation of certain provisions of the Charter under conditions when no other option was left, should lead to the disintegration of the UN, any more than the invasion of Cuba, which was permitted to be organized on U.S. soil both against the Batista regime as also against its successor, the Castro regime. The end may have been laudable and desirable but were the means adopted not a violation of the Charter? India too can with some justification be blamed for adopting wrong means, e.g., force, to achieve the right end, namely elimination of the last vestiges of colonialism. The Portuguese, on the other hand, in violating the provisions of Article 73, were not only working for the wrong end, viz., continued colonial domination, but in the process were also using wrong means, viz., ruthless suppression and mass killing of the people in their colonial territories. One would have thought that when both means and ends were wrong, the Portuguese should have come in for much more severe criticism than the Indians. In fact, however, they did not come in for any criticism at all, or, if they did get criticized occasionally, it was nothing compared to the criticism that was leveled at India. If the Portuguese violations which are of a worse character do not threaten the existence of the UN, why should Indian action in Goa have that effect?

Indeed, the immediate beneficiary of Indian action in Goa was Indonesia, which got control of West New Guinea through peaceful negotiations. All credit is due to the United States for the initiative it took in arranging for this peaceful transfer of the territory from the Netherlands to Indonesia. We in India felt that our action in Goa, instead of damaging the UN as was feared, had the contrary effect of encouraging the peaceful settlement of at least one other dispute. A Dutchman, however, bitterly complained against the United States for letting the Netherlands down and forcing it to agree to the transfer of West New Guinea to Indonesia under the threat of a military action. He pointed out the inconsistency between the American attitude toward Indian action in Goa and that toward the Indonesian threat to West New Guinea. He said that while Goa was at least geographically a part of India and the people were Indian by race, religion, language and culture, West New Guinea was separated from the rest of the Indonesian islands by a long stretch of the sea, and the inhabitants, the Papuans, were entirely different from other Indonesians ethnically, linguistically and culturally. Americans strongly condemned the Indian taking over of Goa but they actively helped Indonesians in taking over West New Guinea. He cynically observed that, unlike Portugal, Netherlands had no bases to offer. I tried to argue with him by pointing out that a peaceful settlement of this long-standing problem should have been welcome to the Dutch, particularly when they were getting no advantage by hanging on to West New Guinea. In fact, they were spending a lot of money, and were in addition having bad relations with the Indonesians. His retort was that appeasement under a threat of force is more likely to whet the appetite of the Indonesians for other adventures. In retrospect, it seems that he was not perhaps entirely wrong. The "crush Malaysia" policy of Indonesia followed soon after the peaceful transfer of West New Guinea.

The support of the Goa action by Africans and Asians in general is often cited as an example of a "double standard." As I have already tried to explain, India's action in Goa came in for caustic criticism in the Western world, and the same action received approval in Asian and African countries, not because of any double standard, but because of a difference in outlook. The Representative of the United States in a reminiscent mood said that "the League of Nations died when its members no longer resisted the use of aggressive force," * and he predicted that the failure of the Security Council to call for a cease-fire in Goa could end with the death of the UN organization. He was presumably comparing Indian action in Goa with Mussolini's attack on Ethiopia or with Japan's taking over Manchuria. Such a comparison is indeed a very good example of a double standard. Action in Goa was taken to remove the last vestige of colonialism on Indian soil, and to free the remaining section of our own people from oppressive colonial rule. The object of Mussolini's action was just the opposite—to bring Ethiopia under Italian colonial domination. It was the League's desire to have peace at any price, irrespective of any consideration for the principles of

* 988th meeting of the Security Council held on December 18, 1961.

justice, that led to its disintegration. To support Portugal on Goa would have been to support the principle of peace at any price without any reference to the considerations of justice.

One may well recall the prophetic words uttered in the Council of the League of Nations by His Imperial Majesty the Emperor of Ethiopia. Speaking on behalf of the British Government at the 5th meeting of the 101st session of the Council of the League of Nations held on May 12, 1938, Lord Halifax referred to the "resolution adopted by the League in 1932 in the case of 'Manchukuo' upon the subject of nonrecognition of the results of aggressive action" and said that "in that resolution it was agreed by all members of the League that they would not recognize any situation, treaty or agreement which was brought about by means contrary to the Covenant and if we desire to be honest with ourselves and with our fellow-members of the League, we must not be afraid squarely to face the fact in the light of that expression of opinion." Lord Halifax also said that "there are many . . . who feel that . . . any action designed to facilitate recognition of the Italian conquest does impinge on principle, and who would therefore deplore the adoption of such a course. I respect, but I cannot share, their view." He added that "when, as here, two ideals are in conflict—on the one hand the ideal of devotion, unflinching but unpractical, to some high purpose; on the other, the ideal of a practical victory for peace— I cannot doubt that the stronger claim is that of peace."

The Emperor of Ethiopia was present at the meeting of the Council but as he was in a weak state of health, his statement was read by his chief delegate Ato Taezaz. Commenting on the statement of Lord Halifax, the Emperor said:

"True! The essential object of the League is to maintain peace. But there are two ways of maintaining peace; there is the maintenance of peace through right and there is peace at any price. Ethiopia is profoundly convinced that the League of Nations has no freedom of choice. It would be committing suicide if, after having been created to maintain peace through right, it deserted that principle for the principle of peace at any price even by the immolation of a State Member at the feet of its aggressor."

The outbreak of World War II so soon thereafter proved how right he was. Having failed to act in accordance with the principles of justice and attempting to maintain peace at any price, the League could neither prevent World War II nor its own disintegration. It is essential to keep this fact always before us lest the United Nations go the same way as did the League of Nations. Mussolini's attack on Ethiopia would have been comparable if India had attacked the mainland of Portugal with a view to bringing it under Indian colonial domination. In that case, the Indian action would certainly have brought outright condemnation from Africans and Asians alike. If, even in those circumstances, they failed to condemn India, it would have been correct to accuse them of "double standard."

I have referred to the statements made in the Security Council by the American Representative because they are on record and can be readily verified.* This reference to his statements is not to suggest, however, that the views expressed by him were only his own. Of course, they represented the views of his government. What is more, the press and public in America gave expression to the same views and made the same criticism. This universal condemnation by Americans was least expected by Indians and that is why it hurt them all the more.

Last but not least, we have been accused of not having

* 987th and 988th meeting of the Security Council held on December 18, 1961.

lived up to our own professions of nonviolence. We are told that the images of India and of Jawaharlal Nehru have been tarnished. Now, what were these images? We do not know what respect and admiration we had before the action in Goa, and what we lost thereafter. In the West, India was sneeringly referred to as a neutralist country, sitting on the fence. That certainly was not a mark of respect or of admiration. As Prime Minister Nehru said to the press on December 28, 1961, "It is very gratifying to see how we are, now, told what a fine image of India there was before the Goa action! The image has been affected! What an unusually great man Nehru was if he had not fallen now! It is something to be told that one was great even if one is not great now." The same newspapers which had criticized Nehru in the past, and which had charged him with hypocrisy, were, after the Goa incident, saying that his image had been tarnished. He had never commanded respect in these quarters and there was nothing he could lose, so far as their opinion was concerned. The respect that he undoubtedly commanded in other quarters was not lost. It is the loss of respect from this quarter that would have mattered.

We certainly claim to be a peaceful people, but we never said that we would never take recourse to force when the door to all peaceful methods of persuasion or negotiation is permanently barred. Nobody had made the position clearer than Prime Minister Nehru who, in the course of a debate in the Indian Parliament in February 1956, had said: "I am not aware of our Government having ever said that they adopted the doctrine of *Ahimsa* to our activities. They may respect it, they may honor that doctrine, but as a Government it is patent what we do not adopt and we do not consider ourselves capable of adopting the doctrine of *Ahimsa.*" We had also made it quite clear in the earlier part of 1961 that the use of force could not be altogether ruled out in the specific case of Goa. In August 1961, speaking in the Parliament, the Prime Minister had said that his government "would vary that policy [about Goa] if necessary or desirable to do so," adding that "the time may come when the army have to march into Goa and the Indian Government" may have to deal with the Goan situation on an "armed basis." It is not therefore our fault if the West for any reason had believed that we would remain nonviolent under all circumstances. It was, I believe, Abraham Lincoln who said, "We love peace but we love liberty the more." Likewise, we Indians say, "We love peace but we love liberty and justice the more."

It is difficult to find an exact English equivalent for the Sanskrit word *Ahimsa*. I would not attempt to explain the doctrine of *Ahimsa*, beyond saying that the nearest English equivalent for the word *Ahimsa* would be action "without malice," and not "nonviolence." The question when and in what circumstance force can be justified can best be answered by quoting what the eminent evangelist Billy Graham said in reply to a question that was put to him. By a strange coincidence, the question and the answers were published in the Ottawa *Citizen* on January 3, 1962, soon after the Indian action in Goa:

QUESTION: Some faiths believe that it is not right to take up arms. What is your stand on the subject? What is their scriptural backing?

ANSWER: Those who do not believe in taking up arms have several scriptures to buttress their point of view. The one most often used is Jesus' words: "They that take the sword shall perish by the sword." (Matt. 26:52)

However there is a vast difference between offensive and defensive warfare. In the scriptural

ethic there are admonitions to "defend" the innocent. The Psalms say: "Defend the poor and fa-
therless; do justice ... deliver the poor and the
needy; rid them out of the hand of the wicked."

Policemen are not aggressive; their purpose is
to defend and protect the innocent, and sometimes, they must "lay hold" of the wicked. Justice
is something we can't easily rule out of the uni-
verse.

We must not be adamant when tyranny threatens the freedom of the innocent. We must not be
indifferent when the weak are oppressed. Jesus
could have prayed for the merchants who defiled
the temple, but He elected to use a lash to cleanse
it of intruders and thieves. There are times when
we must prayerfully and compassionately defend
the needy.

Can anyone, in this view, reasonably accuse India of having
tarnished her image in rescuing her own people in Goa from
the tyranny of the alien Portuguese rulers? Can India be
expected to be more peaceful than the Prince of Peace?

DEMOCRACY IN INDIA

WHILE many American friends of India consider India as the principal bastion of democracy outside Europe and North America, there are quite a few skeptics who would shake their heads and doubt if democracy can flourish at all in India. India has disappointed many a prophet of gloom who had predicted that it would disintegrate completely soon after the British left. When that did not happen, all credit for keeping democracy going in India went to Nehru alone, and doubts were expressed that the so-called democracy in India would fail once Nehru disappeared from the Indian scene. It then became fashionable not only to ask "After Nehru who?" but also "After Nehru what?" Nehru was criticized for not even indicating a possible successor. The fact was ignored that in a democracy it would be most unusual for a Prime Minister to earmark his successor. As Mr. Nehru had told a New York audience in November 1961, the grooming of a successor had seldom been done in a democracy, and when it was attempted in a recent case, it had proved to be a failure. The fear that after the death of Nehru, democracy in India might be replaced by some form of dictatorship also proved unfounded. When Mr. Lal Bahadur Shastri succeeded Mr. Nehru in the normal democratic manner, the question that was immediately raised is "How long can Shastri last?"

It is this sort of doubts, particularly when accompanied by smiles and sneers, that irritates the Indian who is perhaps unduly sensitive on this subject. American fear, often unconcealed, that India may move, or is moving, toward Communism adds to this annoyance. To describe secular India wrongly as Hindu India in the context of the Islamic State of Pakistan, as so many Americans do, appears to most Indians as a deliberate slur on the liberal provisions included in their Constitution. The Indian cannot understand that Americans who speak on these lines often do so out of ignorance. Instead of getting annoyed, Indians should try to point out the facts which might help in dispelling such ignorance.

Americans cannot be blamed too much if they are still somewhat skeptical about the prospects of democracy thriving in India, when they see new democracies all around India falling down like ninepins. They had seen frequent failures of democracy in Latin America, often replaced by dictatorial regimes. They were therefore inclined to question the nature of the democracies established in newly independent countries. Their doubts were only confirmed when they found so many countries, which started with democratic forms of government, ending up in a few years with some form of authoritarian rule. Many newly independent countries, in the first flush of independence, adopted the democratic institutions which prevailed in the metropolitan territories of the colonial rulers. The failure of such institutions at a later date can be attributed to different reasons. Certain factors, however, seem to be common in all cases. Lack of real national unity sometimes threatens disruption and only an authoritarian regime can prevent disintegration. Another basic reason for the failure of democracy has been the apathy of the masses toward democratic institutions, due to illiteracy, poverty and lack of any desire to fight for their rights.

The failure of democracy in newly independent countries has generally led either to a military dictatorship or to a one-party system of government. In the view of West Europeans and North Americans, both changes amount to erosion of democracy. There is hardly anyone who can convincingly argue that military dictatorship can still claim to be a form of democracy. Many countries, particularly in Africa, however, claim that democracy need not necessarily adopt a parliamentary system of government; nor must a democracy necessarily have an opposition party. Many of these countries have gone in for a one-party system of government on the ground that this type of government is better suited to the genius of their people, and is appropriate in their circumstances. The most urgent need for such countries, it is argued, is national integration and economic development. They cannot afford, at this stage, to fritter away their energies in fighting elections and squabbling among themselves. They must direct all their efforts to consolidation and development. The luxury of having an opposition can be considered only after these immediate objectives are achieved. A one-party system can still be a democratic form of government. After all, in wartime, many Western democracies also have had national coalition governments. Developing countries should be on a similar war footing in their fight against poverty and disease.

Many, or at least some, of these arguments seem in American eyes also to apply to India and they somewhat naturally wonder if there is really any democracy in India and, if so, how long can it last before it fails, as it has failed in so many other countries. It is true that there is poverty and mass illiteracy in India, but then, we have also a large middle class, which is the backbone of any democracy. Our history, our tradition, our religion, all teach tolerance which is one of the essential prerequisites of democracy. We have also had a fair degree of industrial development and this has led to the growth of a sizable organized labor force. Unlike agricultural labor which has often to depend on the forces of nature, industrial labor is much more self-reliant, for it knows the important role it plays in running the machinery. The industrial labor knows its power, its rights, and often fights for them. This, then, is a good breeding ground for democracy.

We have also been lucky in having a well-trained Civil Service and having our armed forces used to civilian control. The greatest good fortune that we had was to have as national leader, for nearly seventeen years, a man like Nehru who had an undisputed sway over the people. With such a commanding personality on the scene, the armed forces had no temptation to try to seize political power. The tradition of accepting civilian control thus continued even after independence and is now well established.

Many Americans who have visited India have had their doubts about Indian democracy thoroughly dispelled. Three years ago, I read an article written by Professor Clinton Rossiter on what he called "The Paradox of India's Democracy." * He came to the conclusion that democracy does exist in India despite the fact that "almost none of the alleged prerequisites

* *The New York Times,* June 3, 1962 (Magazine Section).

of democracy exists to any marked degree in that country." He has analyzed the causes of this apparent paradox with sympathy and great ability. It is not necessary for me to quote extensively from the article of Professor Rossiter. If I am referring to his article it is only to satisfy the Indian reader that well-informed Americans do not berate Indian democracy and that he need not be unduly sensitive on the subject. It is the absence of some of the so-called prerequisites of democracy that raises doubts in American minds, particularly when in apparently similar circumstances, democratic institutions disappeared from some of the newly independent countries.

The fact that the Congress Party has retained so dominant a position in India, and for so long, has given rise to an impression among a section of Americans—not so well informed—that India has also succumbed to a one-party government. Obviously, they do not know that there are a number of parties which run candidates in opposition to the ruling Congress Party, that the total votes secured by all the opposition parties combined have more than equaled those cast in favor of the candidates of the Congress Party. It is because of the existence of so many splinter parties among the opposition that no single party has so far been able to challenge the huge majority of the Congress Party. The opposition votes have to be shared by three or four parties, and in such triangular or quadrangular contests, the Congress Party has been able to win many more seats than would otherwise be justified by the total votes secured by it. Attempts to unite the opposition parties into one strong party have so far failed mainly because the opposition parties are either to the extreme right or to the extreme left.

This section of American opinion which looks with suspicion upon the continuance of one party in power so long in

India has apparently forgotten how long the Democratic Party ruled the United States despite the existence of the well-organized Republican Party. Next door in Canada, the Liberal Party was in power for well over twenty years before the Progressive Conservative Party could get a chance to defeat it at the polls. The Indian Congress Party started with a tremendous prestige—the prestige of having secured the independence of the country through nonviolent means. In all three elections held so far, the party also had the good fortune of being led by an outstanding personality like Jawaharlal Nehru, ably assisted by a number of other national leaders who had established their reputation during the national struggle for independence. Is it then any wonder that the electorate should have continued to favor the Congress Party so long? Now that Nehru is no more and so many of the Congress Party leaders of all-India stature are dead, the party will no doubt have greater difficulty in retaining the large majority that it has enjoyed in the Parliament so long. All this explains why the Congress Party has been able so long to hold such a dominant position and there can be no reason to accuse the Congress Party of leading India to a system of one-party government.

American doubts as to the functioning of a genuine democracy in India also stem from some other popular misconceptions. One is that India is a Hindu state just as Pakistan is an Islamic state, and that the treatment of the minorities by the majority community is much the same in both countries. This popular belief among Americans annoys and irritates the Indian. India never accepted the Pakistani theory that Moslems and Hindus are two different nations. Indians are justifiably proud of their Constitution, setting up a secular state in which no special favor is accorded to any community and in which everyone is entitled to profess and practice his religion without let or hindrance from the state. There is no sphere of our national activity where Moslems and other minorities do not hold important positions—positions of responsibility. In Pakistan, non-Moslems are not only statutorily deprived of the birthright of every natural-born citizen to hold the highest office in the state, but they are also subjected to political and economic discrimination and are left with a constant sense of insecurity. As a result, non-Moslems are leaving their hearths and homes and migrating to India in large numbers. This is clearly proved by the Pakistani Census figures for the years 1951 and 1961. According to these figures, there were 9.24 million non-Moslems in 1951. The corresponding figure for 1961 is 9.38 million. The non-Moslem population in Pakistan has remained practically stationary, although the increase in the population of Moslems during the decade has been 26 percent. With a similar percentage of increase, the non-Moslem population should have gone up by over 2.25 million. If there has been no such increase, it is because approximately that number of non-Moslems had to migrate to India as refugees. The Indian Census figures for 1961, on the other hand, show that there has been an increase of 25.6 percent in the population of Moslems in India during the period 1951–61 against an overall increase in the population of India of 21.5 percent. Despite these facts, to say that the treatment of minorities in the two countries is much the same is taken as an affront by the Indian. He does not realize that few Americans are aware of these facts and that they are carried away by the vague impression that India was partitioned into Hindustan and Pakistan on the basis of religion. The fact that India has fifty million Moslem citizens and is the third largest Moslem country is perhaps known only to few Americans. India is a secular state. It could not be otherwise with 50 million

Moslems, 12 million Christians and 20 million professing other faiths. In India we are proud to have some of the earliest Christians in the world. St. Thomas, the Apostle of Christ, came to India in the first century A.D. The descendants of the people whom he converted to Christianity live today in South India and his own remains are buried in Saint Thomas Mount, near Madras.

Americans also find it difficult to understand how democracy can flourish in an India which they believe to be still completely caste-ridden. In their ignorance, they believe that caste controls all aspects of life in India and, as such, there can be no democratic equality. They do not know that caste does not nowadays affect the political or economic life in any way even though admittedly caste still counts in the social life of the people in some backward areas. In the course of one of my addresses before a group of university students, one student said that he had heard two contradictory views about the role played by the caste system in the economic development of India. One view, he said, was that caste helps economic development and the other view was that it hinders such development. He asked me which of these assertions is correct in my view. I had to explain that neither view is really correct since caste plays no significant role in modern economic developments that are taking place in India. In a factory, or in an industrial plant, no one knows what the caste of the employee is. The agriculturists who constitute three quarters of the population belong to all religions and castes. The only sphere where caste may be of some importance is in cottage industries such as handloom weaving or other village handicrafts. The know-how in handicrafts is still generally passed on from father to son, or at any rate is mostly restricted to particular castes, e.g., the weaver, the blacksmith, the goldsmith, the carpenter, etc. Even this system is now breaking down because of the training given in cottage industries in different schools to young people, irrespective of caste or creed. Except in some villages, cottage industries are no longer absolutely restricted to any particular castes. In some private industries, members of particular communities which had specialized in certain types of business, e.g., Marwaris Bhatias, Parsees, etc., used to monopolize certain trades. This is not, however, peculiar to India; there are similar types of family business in Europe and America. Jewish business houses are good examples. This sort of family business is disappearing in India for the same reasons as in Europe and America, and is being gradually replaced by joint stock companies.

There are many countries in the world where discrimination in one form or another does exist. Passions or prejudices continue, and sometimes antisocial elements succeed in exploiting them, particularly in a society where the vast majority of the population is still illiterate and ignorant. We all recognize it as evil, we are ashamed of it, we fight against it and organize public opinion against it. This we have done intensively ever since Mahatma Gandhi took up the cause of the untouchables, whom he called "Harijans"—children of God. Since our independence we have tried to eradicate the evils of casteism and communalism by special legislation and we have succeeded in a great measure in doing so. If we have not yet had 100 percent success, this is because social evils die hard, and it takes time to rouse social conscience. Americans should appreciate this difficulty, for they themselves are finding it difficult to eradicate racialism in their country despite legislation and Supreme Court decisions. We admire the genuine efforts that Americans are making toward the eradication of racial discrimination, particularly because their action is in refreshing contrast to the situation in South Africa where racial discrimination is not only condoned but is even encouraged by the government as a state policy. Our efforts to eradicate casteism and communalism should be equally appreciated in the United States.

Americans are still suspicious about India's relationship with the Communist world. Nehru was considered by quite a significant section of American opinion as a crypto-Communist. Our advocacy of peaceful coexistence, our championing of the representation of Communist China in the UN and our expressed desire to create a socialistic pattern of society, raise doubts in the American mind as to whither India is going. There should be no reason for such doubts. We ourselves have made our choice and we have opted for a parliamentary democracy. We have no quarrel with Communist countries so long as they do not attempt to interfere in our internal affairs. We do not believe that Communism as such is necessarily hostile to us. The Communist Chinese invaded India in 1962, but most other Communist states openly showed their sympathy with India in this conflict. The Soviet Union took a neutral attitude immediately after the Chinese attack on India, with an initial bias in favor of the People's Republic of China. Soon after, however, the Soviet Union offered us some military help to strengthen our defense against the Communist Chinese. We have therefore no reason to blame Communism for the Chinese attack on us. Soviets have also given us support on some other issues of vital national interest to us, particularly on Kashmir and Goa. All this friendliness from the Soviets has been appreciated in India and there is naturally a considerable volume of goodwill toward the Soviet Union notwithstanding their different system of government, which they have not asked us to adopt nor do we have any desire to imitate.

What are the dangers of India going Communist? It would be dogmatic to assert that there is no such possibility at all. On the other hand, the risk, if any, has been highly exaggerated in the U.S.A. It must be remembered that among the newly admitted members of the United Nations Organization, none has so far changed over to a Communist government. These new countries may have varying degrees of friendship with the Communist world, but by and large, they have chosen to remain nearer to the form of government of their erstwhile colonial rulers and even when they have had to give up the form of democracy of the West European pattern because of their own problems and requirements, the form of government is nowhere similar to those of the East European countries. One reason for this is that the newly independent countries are more familiar with the system they had seen working in the metropolitan areas of their colonial rulers. They have no similar knowledge of the form of government in the East European countries.

The attraction of Communism as a creed must not, however, be entirely overlooked. The appeal of Communism as a shortcut to achieving economic wonders should not be belittled. The rapid economic development brought about in the comparatively backward areas of the Soviet Union and the advance made by the People's Republic of China are the envy of the underdeveloped world. The much faster rate of growth in Japan is ignored because it was already industrially advanced. Similarly the development in Formosa is attributed to the massive economic aid received from the U.S.A. The per capita grant-in-aid in Formosa is beyond the dream of other underdeveloped countries. It is because of this appeal for the totalitarian method of development that we in India are so anxious to ensure that our five-year plans succeed. If our democratic methods of development fail, there is of course the risk that the pressure for the alternative—the total-itarian—method might be too great to resist.

The comparatively few Communists that we have in India come, strangely enough, not so much from the poorer peasants and laborers as from the frustrated intelligentsia—students and the middle class. The peasants and the laborers living in villages do not as yet have much reason for envying their fellow citizens, most of whom share their lot. Until wants are created and they get acutely dissatisfied with their standard of living, propaganda for a violent revolution is not likely to succeed among them, particularly as they are fortunately still religious-minded. So long as our development plans bring about a steady rise in the standard of living, the danger of the masses being incited to violence is minimal. The intelli-gentsia, however, notices and envies the comparatively higher standard of living of the more affluent and the well-to-do. It is this class that feels frustrated, finds no solace in religion and clamors for more material comforts. One cannot say whether Communism appeals to them because of its idealism or because they believe in its methods. One thing, however, is certain and that is that unless the problem of educated unemployment can be controlled, Communism will have the greatest appeal to the middle-class intelligentsia.

INDIANS AND AMERICANS

I F one looks below the surface, there is considerable similarity in the character of Indians and Americans. Like many other people, both want to be loved and both are extremely sensitive to criticism. Indians belonging to every stratum of life feel hurt when something unfavorable to India is published in American books, newspapers and periodicals. It is quite common for Indians to complain when well-known American newspapers and periodicals write articles critical of India. It is equally common for Americans to quote from some of the leftist press in India criticizing the U.S.A. Americans and Indians while complaining about these criticisms against themselves forget that there is a free press in both countries and there is nothing in law that stands in the way of anybody giving vent to his feelings or expressing his views freely; nor do they remember that while some journals or periodicals may criticize, others do not. I think Indians and Americans both place undue importance on what is said in newspapers and periodicals. A newspaper or a periodical has its own policy and it is often tempted to present facts with a little twist to fit them in with their policy. That may not be entirely ethical or very desirable but these are the realities of life which should not be ignored.

It is indeed a sad commentary on our times that steady and sustained efforts for the betterment of human society receive but little publicity. On the other hand, anything sensational, anything unusual, hits the headlines. Every newspaper has its own appreciation of what has news value. I have noticed that thought-provoking and constructive statements in the United Nations made by delegates of small countries are often completely blacked out while critical remarks made by some other delegates of similar standing are given a great deal of prominence in the American press, because they are supposed to have some news value. This type of coverage of sensational news is of course not entirely the fault of the newspapers. They have to supply it in response to the demand of the reading public. The public apparently cares more for sensational news, comic strips and local scandals than for serious or heavy reading. Newspapers or periodicals would go broke if they did not cater to the demands of their readers. All this leads to a vicious circle. The reader gets used to juicy stories and he will not read anything that does not fit in with or contradicts the misleading stories on which he may have been fed in the past. It is news to show the seamy side of Indian life and that is what many readers have gotten accustomed to read. Any departure from that type of writing appears to be somewhat odd to the average reader. There is therefore still the undue emphasis on the worst features of the caste system without taking the trouble to point out, at the same time, the steps that have been or are being taken to eradicate this evil. It is not often that one sees articles describing the economic developments that are taking place in India or the improvements that are being brought about on the social side. Hardly any publicity is given to democratic practices in India. Much more is said about the weaknesses in Indian democracy—real or imaginary. Apparently many newspapers and periodicals do not think that such articles would be of any interest to the average reader. Newspapers and periodicals thus help in perpetuating the ignorance of the reader, which in its turn leads to a lack of interest on his part.

This is not to say that all American newspapers and periodicals succumb to the temptation of yielding to the wishes of their readers. There are many exceptions. I am, however, referring to this aspect of the problem only to assure the Indian reader that the articles critical of India are not necessarily written with malice or even with the knowledge that such articles damage Indo-American relations. I have read many excellent articles in the American newspapers and periodicals on India which show a great deal of careful study. One may not always agree with the views expressed but one has to admire the trouble taken to understand the problems.

Newspapers and periodicals, particularly those with large circulations, exercise very great influence on the average reader and often help to mold his opinions. This is true not only in respect to people in India but also the better-educated people in the United States. I recall an evening in October 1961 when after a strenuous day in the UN I had gone out for dinner in a restaurant with another member of the Indian delegation. We had had an excellent dinner and we were at peace with the world and were enjoying our after-dinner coffee and cigarettes, when two couples at the next table started a friendly conversation with us. In course of the conversation we were suddenly asked why we were acting against the interests of the U.S.A. by trying to stop the resumption of nuclear tests by Americans when the Soviets had already broken the moratorium. I pointed out that we wanted to stop all nuclear testing. I tried to explain that if our draft resolution were to be promptly adopted by the General Assembly it would be the Soviets who would be embarrassed. They would have to stop the tests which they had resumed or if they continued to carry on the tests they would do so by flouting the world public opinion as reflected in the resolution. I was told that the newspapers were giving a different story. I suggested that if they gave me their address, I would send them the verbatim records of the First Committee which would show exactly what the Indian delegation had been asking for. The offer did not evoke any interest. I was asked if I considered *The New York Times* to be a good newspaper. On receiving a reply in the affirmative, they said that they regularly read *The New York Times* and that I should then agree that something which *The New York Times* did not publish could not be worth reading! I was disappointed to find that there were some even among educated Americans who preferred to remain ignorant of things that *The New York Times* might not find it possible to cover. One would have normally expected them to welcome reliable information, but they were apparently unwilling to learn.

Many Indians complain that while American newspapers and periodicals write about the darker side of Indian social and political life, they never do so in regard to Pakistan where the conditions are much the same as in India. These Indians seem to forget that India is a much larger country, has greater news value and that because of these reasons there is a much larger coverage of India in American newspapers and periodicals than of most non-European countries. This should be taken rather as a compliment in so far as the comparatively large coverage is an indication of the importance that is attached to India—an importance which Americans deny to many other countries. It may be true that the articles written on India in American newspapers and magazines are often critical and unsympathetic. Even the factual news is sometimes reported with an unfavorable slant. Personally I believe that antipathy is at least better than complete apathy. Before showing an antipathy one must notice the existence of the object of antipathy. Apathy implies complete indifference. I would feel much more hurt if we were altogether ignored, for that would give the impression that we were not even worth noticing. Therefore, although most Indians resent this critical and unsympathetic coverage, I myself find some satisfaction in seeing that we are at least important enough to be noticed even though notice is more often taken only of the darker side of our life.

There are plenty of well-written books on India. Also there are many books, the authors of which find nothing good in India. Most Indians feel hurt when they read the latter kind of books and they automatically assume that the particular book was intended to be an affront to them. That is not always or necessarily the case. The author visits India for a few weeks or months and feels impelled to write an authoritative book on India. He may have been appalled by the poverty, squalor and filth that he finds in India. That shock takes away all his objectivity and he thinks that everything in India is bad. He writes about the distorted image that he sees, not necessarily because he loathes India, but perhaps because he thinks he is making a great discovery. We in India have raised no wall of secrecy around us. We have an open society and everything good or bad is there for everyone to see. There are of course many things bad in India, many problems which still baffle any satisfactory solution. But is there any country where something bad or dirty cannot be found? It is the undue emphasis on these dirty things alone that gives a distorted picture of India. If one were to write a monograph on the United States on the basis of the records of the criminal courts or of what happens in the underworld of dope, sex and juvenile delinquency, that might be justified if it were intended to be a scientific study of some specific aspects of life in the country. That would be a study of the aberrations one can find in the U.S.A. or, for the matter of that, in many other countries. It would be wrong however to give the impression that that is what the real America is or to claim that there is nothing else in America. It is books that give such impressions or make such absurd claims that one can and must condemn. A book written with the specific object of making a scientific study of a particular aberration should not only not hurt anyone but should be welcome in so far as it presents a problem which needs a speedy solution.

Sometimes authors prefer to write a sensational or controversial book because they feel that such a book would have a more extensive sale than a scientific study which would interest only the specialist. In writing a book the author often reveals his own mind and incidentally shows what exactly interests him in the country—good or bad. Visitors often look at new places and at strange customs with preconceived ideas and sometimes through jaundiced eyes. Few writers succeed in writing an objective account of the country they visit, giving a balanced account of both the good and the bad that they see. The temptation is often to write either only about the seamy side of life or only the good side of it. One should not therefore take too seriously all the unpleasant things that visitors may write about India. What is written can seldom be brushed aside as totally incorrect. More often the book is written on the basis of some facts which may have been distorted either through some misunderstanding or for some other reason. Visitors sometimes show remarkable credulity and are often gullible enough to accept anything that they hear, without any critical examination. This is specially noticeable in the writings of those who visit a new country with preconceived notions, sometimes good, sometimes bad. Anything that fits in with such notions is automatically accepted without further scrutiny. Anything that does not fit in is taken as an exception, deviating from the normal. It never occurs to them that what they accept as normal may well be the exception and vice versa. In every country there are people who are against the government or other established authority. That is not a characteristic which by any means is a monopoly of the Irish even though this trait is so often associated with them. While the views of such people should not be ignored, it would be wrong to give the impression that their opinions alone are necessarily correct because they happen to coincide with the writer's own preconceived notions.

As to the credulity of some writers, I can do no better than quote what a visitor said after visiting India. This visitor—who is an American—found almost everything wrong in India and spoke disparagingly of everything that he had noticed in India. He conceded that the one thing that had impressed him during his entire stay in India was the uniform courtesy of the bearded and turbaned Sikh taxi driver in Delhi. He was however disillusioned when he found out the real reason for this apparent courtesy. He said that whenever he hailed a cab driver, the driver stopped the car, got down, opened the door to let him get into the cab, and similarly when he wanted to get out, the cab driver would again get out of the car and politely open the door to let him out. This was a courtesy he had never received from cab drivers in North America or Europe and he was therefore most impressed. But lo and behold—this courtesy proved to be entirely an illusion when he asked one such Sikh driver to explain why he acted in that way. The Sikh driver perhaps had a sense of humor, and he is reported to have told the visitor that when someone hails the cab, he is anxious to push him inside the car before he can change his mind and that is why he gets out to open the door. Again, when the client wants to get out, he opens the door and stands there to prevent him from running away without paying the fare! Can there be a more ludicrous explanation? Yet the visitor who was determined not to find anything good in India swallowed this explanation, hook line and sinker. This is perhaps an extreme example but there are many such amusing stories in books written about India.

Unfavorable books and articles are often written about India through ignorance and misunderstanding. They are sometimes written by well-meaning people who wish to rouse sympathy for the poverty and misery they notice in India. That being so, we should not ourselves uncritically jump to the conclusion that all these writings are by people who are definitely anti-Indian. We should examine the criticism contained in the book. If it is justified we should try to remedy those defects. A foreigner can sometimes see defects which we cannot see ourselves because we are so used to them. If, on the other hand, the criticism is obviously the result of some misunderstanding, we should make every effort to remove those misunderstandings to the extent possible. If there is no basis whatsoever for the criticism, we can only shrug our shoulders and ignore it, conceding the democratic right of everyone to say what he likes. That is the only way one can keep one's balance. There is no point in being unduly emotional or being intolerant of criticism. This applies as much to Indians as to Americans—perhaps more so to Americans. Indian intolerance to criticism does not perhaps affect others so much, since the fact that we are annoyed is not of much consequence to the world. American intolerance to criticism may make them, in their annoyance, take some action in haste which they may regret later and which may hurt the country concerned against which such action is taken. It must be remembered that a leader is always destined to be criticized violently and sometimes even unfairly. Any action taken by Americans as leaders of the free world affects not only Americans or even only their allies but also a great part of the world. Americans feel that having given general economic help to so many countries, they have a right to expect that at least the people of these countries would show some gratitude by not criticizing them. It is wrong to expect such gratitude. In a free society, friends must criticize if only to prevent rash and unwise actions being undertaken. Americans had quite friendly and cordial relations with the British but that did not prevent Americans from twisting the tail of the British lion whenever they felt it necessary to do so. In this context, one cannot but admire the British capacity to take criticisms in their stride. The seemingly tolerant attitude taken by the British may have stemmed from a superiority complex but, whatever may have been the reason, the tolerance they showed in the heyday of their imperial power should be an object of emulation by the United States now that it happens to be the strongest power in the world today. Let them try to develop the British attitude: "They say. What say they? Let them say." This superciliousness may be irritating but has some distinct advantages, too.

Americans often say—and there may be some truth in what they say—that extreme sensitivity to criticism as shown by the Indian comes from some sort of inferiority complex. The inferiority complex, they say, may have been brought about partly by the racial discrimination suffered by them in the colonial days and partly by their own economic backwardness.

With independence has at least come the realization to Indians that they are in no way inferior to other people. Economic weakness, however, continues, and to cover up this inferiority some Indians speak a little too much about their spiritual heritage. While there is much to be proud of on this account, it looks rather ridiculous for an Indian to talk of spiritualism when in his conduct he shows the worst of materialism. Many Indians irritate people by assuming a superior spiritual attitude when in their actual behavior they show pettiness of mind and lack of generosity. They do not realize that by their conduct they give an impression that they are hypocrites and sanctimonious humbugs. Similar defects can be found also among some Americans who make themselves equally insufferable by the self-righteous conviction with which they often argue their case. Not only will they refuse to yield when arguments go against them but they will sometimes go to the extent of imputing sinister motives to their opponents. They also often talk about high moral principles but fail to act up to them. In fact, it is the similarity between Indians and Americans who take up an attitude of self-righteousness and moral superiority that makes them sometimes dislike one another. This probably accords with the theory that likes repel while opposites attract.

If the Indian suffers from an inferiority complex, perhaps the American also has not yet completely rid himself of the inferiority complex that seems to have been thrust on him by the European trying to impress on him his cultural superiority. Many Europeans, realizing American superiority in other fields, wanted to show off superiority in the cultural field and assumed a contemptuous attitude toward the crude, brash and vulgar colonial who showed his lack of culture by ostentatiously parading his wealth. They talked about empty-headed heiresses, and arrogant business tycoons lacking in social graces. Much of this prejudiced criticism arose from a sense of jealousy and a grudging acceptance of the fact that power has passed on to America. All this is past history now and America is fast increasing its own contribution in the cultural sphere. The European has no longer much reason to feel superior on this account but the complex, once developed, cannot perhaps be got rid of easily.

Americans sometimes complain that Indians lack good manners and are arrogant. Indians say the same about some Americans. There is perhaps some difference in each others' standard as to what correct manners are. In some ways Indians and Americans are similar. They are both extroverts and try to make friends easily. Indians and Americans have not, however, yet had long enough contacts and they are perhaps trying to judge them on the standards they were familiar with in the past. Indians were more familiar with the British who were correct but rather cold in their manners. It took a long time to make an Englishman friendly and communicative. When the American makes himself friendly often in the first encounter, the too great familiarity comes as a surprise to the Indian. Americans, on the other hand, were more accustomed to deal with the Chinese. In the days when Americans knew them—before the advent of Communism—the Chinese were always deferential and often obsequious. Such conduct was the result of the acceptance, over a long period of time, of the superior status of the foreigner. Americans may not know, but similar respect and deference were also shown to Europeans in India. American contact with the Indian increased rapidly only after Indian independence. Americans met mainly Indian intellectuals and were surprised to find that their outspokenness bordered almost on the point of rudeness. Such was also the experience of the British during the last few decades of their rule in India. It was the modern intellectual trained in Europe or America who irritated the British rulers as opposed to the aristocrats who had their old-world charm and a certain amount of obsequiousness. The Indian intellectuals were not prepared to show any such deference. As a reaction against European claim to superiority, they became more aggressive and sometimes even brusque. The Indian must realize that whatever might have been his excuse in the past he can no longer afford to be impolite or discourteous. Outspokenness may be a virtue but one must present his views with courtesy and respect. Now that Indians and Americans are seeing more of one another, it is to be hoped that they will understand more and more their respective manners and customs.

Most Americans, other than those who may have made a special study, find it difficult to understand Hinduism. On one extreme is the highly philosophical concept of a formless infinite God and at the other end is idol worship for those who find it difficult to concentrate on a formless being. In between, there is a baffling variety of religious practices, superstitions and myths. There is nothing like the Bible or the Koran for the Hindu, whose religions scriptures are far too voluminous for an easy study. It is because of these difficulties that many misconceptions have arisen. Mysticism, for instance, is often believed to be a typical Indian product. That is by no means correct. Essential elements of mysticism are common for the Christian, the Sufi, the Indian and the Chinese saint. What is perhaps true is that the influence of mysticism on society has been greater in India than elsewhere. Another popular misconception is that we are obsessed by our preoccupation with metaphysics. Here again, it is undoubtedly true that India has produced many more people interested in the spiritual side of life than many other countries, but it would be a mistake to think that in general we

are any the less materialistic than other people. If our philosophy has been transcendental, we have not been neglectful
of the good things of this earthly life either. Our contributions to arts and sciences, sculptures, architecture and paint-
ings give proof enough of our mundane interests and accom-
plishments.

In the cultural sphere, India first came to be known to the
West through its literature and its philosophy. We owe a
deep debt of gratitude to the many eminent European scholars who placed before Western readers the beauties of the
Sanskrit literature and made them familiar with the high
standards reached by Indian philosophy. India thus came to
be associated only with religion and metaphysics, and the
living realities of its culture were ignored. There was a rude
shock when Indian art was first brought to the notice of
people who had been used to identifying India only with spir-
ituality. Many a critic "recoiled with puritanical shudders"
at the "voluptuous and sensuous" quality of some Indian
sculptures and the "provocative indulgence" of the female
figures. The delicate poses of the female figures, "nimble
waists" and "firm breasts" shocked the critics all the more
as they had visualized India as the land of high philosophy
and austere asceticism. The symbolism of the *Mithuna* figures or the erotic motifs completely baffled most Western
critics. It needed a deep and careful study before they could
understand that the *Mithuna* figures and their embraces typ-
ify the idea of *Moksha* or the final union with God. In one
of our Upanishads there is a text which says that "just as a
man embraced by a beloved woman forgets everything else
inside or outside, so also the soul of man embraced by the
Holy spirit forgets everything else inside or outside." The
embrace of the *Mithuna* figures is meant to symbolize the
union of the soul with God. With an understanding of the

symbolism, came the critics' appreciation of the beauty and the loveliness of the female figures.

The so-called otherworldliness of the Indian is another generalization which is not correct. We have undoubtedly had many people of that type in our long history and have some even today. That is perhaps more than some other countries can boast of. At the same time, it would be absurd to think that most people in India are like that. It is also not true that the Indian culture elevated poverty to an ideal. From the earliest Vedas and the Puranas, the prayers and sacrifices have also been directed toward achieving earthly prosperity. In fact renunciation has been left for the religious teachers who emphasized the virtues of voluntary poverty. For the rest of the society, there was no ban on efforts to achieve material prosperity. It was a Hindu reformer Swami Vivekananda who said: "I do not want a religion which does not wipe the tears off the widow's cheeks and does not provide bread to the orphan's mouth." It is not therefore true to think that the Hindu religion ignored material prosperity. Nor is there any truth in a belief that there is a widespread practice of renunciation of worldly things. We have had perhaps more than our fair share of religious leaders who have taken recourse to renunciation and have shown otherworldliness, but that does not mean that the people of India, by and large, practice renunciation. It is therefore as futile to expect all Indians to behave like Gandhi as it would be to expect all Americans to be Abraham Lincolns. To judge each other on these standards would be completely unrealistic. We do however criticize one another when we fall short of these high standards. We are even expected to run our government on Gandhian principles, which is manifestly impossible. At a luncheon given to him by the National Press Club in Washington on November 9, 1961, Prime Minister

Nehru said, "A saintly person may take up an attitude regardless of consequences. A politician can hardly ever do that. He may aim at the right, he may have perception of the right, but especially in a democratic country, he must convey that perception to others in order to function. A saint need not; therefore, he is often stoned to death and there the matter ends."

There is perhaps some truth in the charge that our poverty and our underdevelopment are due to our religious beliefs. It is true in the sense that the religious beliefs helped in making poverty bearable and encouraged our people to keep their wants to the minimum. Mahatma Gandhi would have liked people to keep their wants to the minimum. He believed that people would then be happy and contented. This is one of the Gandhian ideas which we could never accept. On the contrary, we took to the ideas of Nehru, which were to encourage people to create wants and to develop discontent. These were considered as the essential prerequisites to progress. The Indian villager today is not therefore as reconciled to his lot as he might have been some years ago. Unless we can now meet his demands we may have social upheavals. Indians followed Gandhi in the struggle for freedom but very few among them followed Gandhiism.

Tourists often create a wrong image of their country by their crude and unmannerly behavior. Being away from their own countries, they become completely uninhibited and do things which they would not dream of doing in their own social surroundings. They do so without realizing the damage that they are doing to their own country. Most Indians love to talk and often talk too much. Even when they are not well informed on a topic, they seldom plead ignorance. They do not seem to know that there is nothing wrong in admitting that they are not fully familiar with the subject. By talking carelessly they often cause misunderstandings and sometimes do harm to the country. The Japanese provide a refreshing contrast and are worthy of our emulation. American tourists often suffer from defects similar to those of Indians. Sometimes they show a great deal of superiority complex and throw their weight about. I recall the case of an American lady who on arrival at the Colombo airport was asked by the Customs man to pay duty on one hundred out of the two hundred cigarettes that she was carrying. Ceylon—like India—is one of the few countries in the world which does not allow two hundred cigarettes free of duty. The lady was so annoyed that she came out with a foolish threat that when she returned to America she would see to it that no American aid came to Ceylon! The Customs man retorted: "Thank God, Ceylon does not take a cent of American aid." This was in 1955, a few months before the United States started granting economic aid to Ceylon. It is this type of tourist who unwittingly does a lot of damage to his country.

Americans believe in an egalitarian society. Yet many of the grievances against Americans are often provoked by the favored positions secured for American nationals through commercial or military agreements. The indigenous competitor is naturally annoyed when special privileges are accorded to the American. American sense of equality makes them dislike privileges given to diplomats in their own country but they themselves want similar privileges elsewhere not only for their own diplomats but also for as many other Americans as possible. Extraterritorialism in military bases brings out anti-Americanism on the surface even in such friendly countries as Japan, South Korea, Philippines, Formosa and South Vietnam. As no such privileges exist in India, so far we had no occasion to face similar problems.

The Hindu food habits create a further barrier to developing social contacts with Indians. No other people in the world have the food restrictions which the Hindu observes even when he is out of India. It would have been simple if there were only vegetarians and nonvegetarians. Unfortunately, that is not so. Even among nonvegetarians, some take all kinds of meat, except beef, some take no fish, others take fish but no meat, and so on. Among vegetarians again there are too many types—some not taking eggs, some not taking certain kinds of vegetables. The host gets completely confused by so many variations. It is no use our saying that we do not want any special treatment. The host or the hostess feels embarrassed all the more not knowing what they can offer to the guests. I remember, late one evening, receiving a long-distance call from an American lady living near Boston asking me if I could tell her what food she could offer to two Indian vegetarian guests coming to a meal with her the following day. I was frankly amazed at being asked such a question on the telephone. I did my best by saying that she could entertain the vegetarian guests by offering them bread, butter, milk, cheese, cottage cheese, vegetables, fruits, etc. The lady was however adamant and asked me if I could not tell her how to make a curry. In diplomatic life one is prepared to answer all kinds of questions about one's country but little did I expect, or was I prepared for, a question on the culinary art of India. I however rose valiantly to the occasion and suggested to the lady that she might make a mixed vegetable stew and put some curry powder in it! If she followed my advice, I hope the Indian guests did not find the dish too unpalatable. This incident taught me two lessons. In the first place it showed how hospitable Americans can be and to what length and trouble an American hostess was prepared to go to please her guests. Secondly, it showed me what difficulties foreigners experience in entertaining Indian guests. The fact that we in India also take a great deal of trouble in trying to prepare European food for our foreign guests is hardly a consolation. Perhaps there would be less embarrassment all round if neither side took too much trouble in preparing special types of food.

CONCLUSION

THE differences between Americans and Indians on comparatively minor issues, or differences in the methods followed to achieve the same objectives, should not make either of us oblivious to our basic interests. It is mutual interests which would ultimately determine the basis of a lasting and friendly relation between our two countries. We want to continue as a strong and stable democracy and for this purpose we want to develop our economy, we want a rise in our standard of living and we want to bring about social equality. The U.S.A. recognizes the pivotal role of India in South and Southeast Asia, and the continuance of India as a strong and stable democracy is as much in the global interest of America. The outcome of the conflict between democratic India and Communist China is not only of vital interest to India but also to the United States. If India cannot successfully resist the pressure of Communist China, the whole of South and Southeast Asia will go down to China. Americans can hardly afford to allow the destruction of the largest democracy in the world. It is this danger that has always to be kept in view and averted at all cost. Economic and military aid that comes from the U.S.A. should not be looked upon by anyone as a sheer waste of money but as an insurance against the preservation of India as the bastion of democracy in the region. With reasonable support from friendly countries, India is the only country which is likely to be able to stand up to the aggressive expansionism of the mainland Chinese. It is the only country in the region which is not yet prepared to acknowledge the power proximity of Communist China and to adapt its policies accordingly. That is precisely what the People's Republic of China desires, in the first instance, from all its neighbors.

We have our political differences with the Americans. In certain areas the policies of the two countries will continue to remain different at least for some time to come. We must however both realize that we will have to live with these differences. We must avoid getting excited about such differences and should not exaggerate their importance. Disagreements on comparatively minor issues will have to be tolerated both by India and the United States, particularly when on most of the basic issues there is a community of interest. We should continue in our efforts to narrow the differences further, wherever possible. If we do not succeed, let not the failure disappoint or dishearten us too much. We must both recognize that it is impossible to wipe out all differences but they must not be allowed to come in the way of developing friendly relations between the two countries.

On certain political issues, particularly on racial and colonial issues, some difference of views seems still unavoidable, although there has been a narrowing of the gap between our respective positions. Because of the reluctance of India to support extreme stands on colonial issues, in our anxiety to get the maximum achievable, we are already being charged with having lost our revolutionary zeal. Indian recognition of Malaysia has annoyed the Indonesians so much that the Indonesian *Herald* wrote on February 10, 1965:

> The country which once championed the cause of the Afro-Asian continents in the fight against imperialism, has now become the outstanding apologist and collaborator for "necolim" domination over those very countries.

"Necolim" presumably means neo-colonialist and imperialist. Indonesia is now saying what the People's Republic of China has been charging us with for quite some time. Americans have now bowed down to the wishes of Asians and Africans and have of late been supporting resolutions condemning apartheid. Despite American support to the newly independent African states, they however complain somewhat bitterly that most new capital invested in South Africa is American.

The difference of views is the widest on two issues—American relations with Pakistan and Indian relations with the Soviet Union. Americans cannot understand how Indians can be friendly with them and at the same time can have cordial relations with the Soviets. Many Indians on the other hand believe that on Indo-Pakistan issues the United States will always support Pakistan as against India. They point out, for instance, that even though some American newspapers admitted that Pakistan was the aggressor in the Rann of Kutch in April 1965, or at any rate tried to alter the status quo by force, there was no criticism by the United States of Pakistan, particularly on the use of U.S. arms in the conflict with India. They also believe that Pakistan exercises some sort of veto on American policy toward India. If this belief is correct, it is best to try to live with it since no amount of criticism in India will change the position. If at all, open criticism would only harden the American stand. We should rather try to understand how difficult it is for the United States to get out of certain commitments that it may have entered into through its military alliance with Pakistan. It is not for us to say what the United States should do in case Pakistan has really changed its attitude. That would quite rightly be looked upon as an interference by us in American foreign policy. We do not obviously want to do that since we do not want Americans to interfere in our efforts to strengthen our friendly relations with the Soviets and other socialist countries. We can and we should make diplomatic representations to the United States if its actions imperil our security. We can request Americans to keep that factor in view in implementing their policy. At the same time, we have every right independently to take such measures as may minimize the risk to our security. Whatever may have been the reasons, in the past, the pro-Pakistan attitude of the United States today cannot possibly stem from any importance of Pakistan as a military ally. The United States must have realized long ago that the armed forces of Pakistan are neither likely to be available nor be of any use to it in a conflict with the USSR or with the People's Republic of China. The reason may well be that the friendly overtures of the People's Republic of China to Pakistan are not merely worrying to India but also to the United States. The Chinese have succeeded for the first time in persuading an ally of the United States virtually to break away from its alliances. Not content with that, Communist China is trying now to get Pakistan completely in its own camp. If China succeeds in its efforts, the Chinese sphere of influence will be extended to the Arabian Sea in the west and the Bay of Bengal in the east. The American anxiety not to loosen its ties with Pakistan any further, if that is at all possible, should therefore be understood by India and even appreciated. Whether the United States will succeed in keeping Pakistan away from the Chinese camp is debatable, especially when Pakistan finds it profitable to exploit this fear on the part of Americans. In our own interest, we should wish Americans all success in their efforts to retain enough influence on Pakistan, but not at our expense. Far from deploring U.S. ties with Pakistan, we should welcome them.

Since it is not possible for the United States to remain really neutral on major Indo-Pakistan issues, it would perhaps be helpful if it could at least avoid equating India with Pakistan on every conceivable occasion. The announcement in April 1965 of the cancellation of the visit to the United States of President Ayub and Prime Minister Shastri might or might not have been justified even from the American point of view. Opinions do, however, differ as to the wisdom of canceling the visits in the manner in which it was done. President Ayub's visit was canceled only about ten days before it was due to begin. President Johnson's preoccupation, at the time, with domestic problems and with Vietnam was a plausible enough excuse for the cancellation. The excuse was however too thin in regard to Prime Minister Shastri, whose visit was due to commence six weeks later in June 1965, particularly when the Americans were prepared to go through with the visit of the President of Korea in the middle of May. The U.S. Government obviously thought that President Ayub's visit could not be canceled without canceling Prime Minister Shastri's visit even though it was due to come much later. It was forgotten that while President Ayub had visited the United States several times in the past, this would have been Mr. Shastri's first visit to America. In any case, there was no need—except on the principle of always equating India with Pakistan—to announce the cancellation of the Shastri visit simultaneously. Such an announcement a couple of weeks later—if it had to come—would not have mattered at all from the American point of view but would have hurt Indians far less. This was a quite unnecessary affront to India. Indians have gotten reconciled to the American support for Pakistan on vital Indo-Pakistan issues even though it makes them unhappy but they just do not understand why India, with five times the population, must always be equated with Pakistan.

Americans must similarly reconcile themselves to India having the most friendly ties with the Soviet Union. No amount of American criticism can weaken the cordial relations now existing. The relations between India and the USSR as also with some other East European countries will continue to grow more and more cordial to their mutual benefit. We not only receive a certain amount of economic aid from these countries, but we have also received their unstinted support on several issues of vital national interest to us. Just as we must live with the U.S.-Pakistan alliance, Americans must also live with Indo-Soviet friendship. We must both recognize that an "all or nothing" policy can never succeed.

The postwar American policy in the Far East was based entirely on friendship with Kuomintang China, but when China went down to Communism, the Americans sought to meet the resulting weakness by creating the SEATO alliance, whose main objective was the containment of Chinese Communism. Now that some of the SEATO allies have not only refused to take part in the implementation of this policy, but are even becoming friendly to the People's Republic of China, the SEATO alliance has demonstrably failed to serve its original purpose. Today, if Americans want any real assistance in containing Chinese Communism, they can get it only by giving all support to India. India is never going to be a military ally of the United States. A strong India would, however, immobilize large Chinese armed forces on its northern borders. That in itself is a worthwhile objective. SEATO allies have failed because their interests no longer coincide with those of the United States. So long as China poses a threat to India, it will have to maintain strong enough forces on its northern borders. It is mutual interest and not alliance that makes both the United States and India oppose Chinese expansionism. India cannot and will not consider that Communism, as such, is a menace to its security. India must plead guilty to the charge of having been unrealistic in the past in ignoring the dangers of the aggressive expansionism of the People's Republic of China. Our fond belief that Communist China would continue to be peaceful and friendly has now been dispelled. Mistakes have been made on both sides, but let us not accuse each other of the past mistakes. If we can recognize them now, it is our duty to correct them. Americans should not, however, expect that merely because we have now been disillusioned with Communist China, we should see the danger of Soviet Communism. On the contrary, our experience shows that the two types of Communism are poles apart and are clearly distinguishable. Soviet Communism is willing to allow nonalignment to continue, believes in peaceful coexistence and abhors war. Chinese Communism wants to destroy nonalignment and believes in the inevitability of war, at least for the present. We have no objection to Communism as such although we do not follow it, because we concede the right to everyone to search for truth and economic salvation in his own way. We do not want a regulated world, all thinking alike.

It is not only important for America but also for the other democracies that the United States must preserve its moral values and its respect for the rule of law in the international sphere. Otherwise there will be little to choose between democracy and totalitarianism. U.S. involvement in Vietnam is understandable. Having entered into certain commitments, any withdrawal without assuring a peaceful solution of the problem might have created the impression that American promises are not dependable. Also American presence in Vietnam may have some legal basis and can perhaps be justified on the ground that the South Vietnamese government had asked for the assistance of its American ally. The Soviets had similarly sought to justify their assistance to the Hungarian government in 1956. Hungary was an ally of the Soviet Union, both being members of the Warsaw Pact. The weakness of this line of argument, however, is that the governments concerned would not perhaps have lasted very long but for the intervention of their allies. Whatever may have been the legal basis of American military presence in Vietnam, U.S. intervention in the Dominican Republic at the end of April 1965 is certainly in conflict both with Article 2 of the Charter of the United Nations and Article 17 of the Charter of the Organization of American States which clearly lays down as follows:

> The territory of a State is inviolable; it may not be the object, even temporarily, of military occupation, directly or indirectly, under any grounds whatever.

One can understand the American desire not to have in the Western hemisphere any regime which they consider to be Communist, but that does not give them the right to interfere in the internal affairs of some other country. At a time when the Soviet Union and other East European countries are prepared to respect the integrity and sovereign equality of states, it would be odd if the greatest democracy in the world were to ignore these principles. It is true that the

People's Republic of China has shown nothing but contempt for the principles of international law, but what moral authority could the United States wield if it were also to depart from these principles as soon as they were found inconvenient?

The action in the Dominican Republic has been criticized both inside and outside the United States. It has done a good deal of damage to the reputation of America. The results achieved may not be commensurate with the damage caused. There may be substantial truth in what *The New York Times* said in an editorial on May 15, 1965:

> Whether there ever was genuine danger of a Communist take-over remains unresolved; but the plain effect of the massing of American marines and paratroopers has been to create a powerful surge of anti-Americanism. So assertive is this sentiment now, that Communist elements in the rebel movement have taken a back seat convinced that the United States will do their job for them more effectively than they could themselves.

Such unilateral action by the United States without consulting its Latin-American friends may also antagonize them even though most of them are staunchly anti-Communist. Indian opinion was generally one of regret but it did not seek to embarrass Americans by expressing open condemnation. This attitude is in glaring contrast to the vitriolic criticism leveled at India by almost all important sections of American opinion on its action in Goa. Americans forgot that Goa, after all, was a colony, geographically a bit of India, and has a population which is entirely Indian by race, religion and culture. Americans may not appreciate it but this comparative silence on the part of India on the Dominican intervention has not been well received in many quarters.

It is such actions that arouse suspicion about the objectives of the United States and subject its relations with friendly countries to unbearable strains. Americans may consider that Communism in any form is dangerous and feel that they must fight it irrespective of the real danger that by doing so, they may only be playing into the hands of the People's Republic of China. To many of us this is a greater danger, since China wants to bring back all Communist countries once again under one undisputed leadership—this time of course under the Chinese. We welcome the wind of change that has come in East Europe and the progressive liberalization that has been going on in the post-Stalin era. It would be a pity to reverse this trend. Americans cannot therefore expect our support for such policies of theirs as would only serve the interests of China. Just as we should reconcile ourselves with U.S. ties with Pakistan even if we are still unable to welcome them, Americans should cease to deplore our friendly ties with the Soviet Union. We should both try to be realists and not confuse our basic and vital interests, which we must defend at all costs, with what we may consider desirable. It should be possible to permit some compromise on such nonessential interests. At any rate, the differences in our views as to what is desirable must not be allowed to stand in the way of developing cordial relations, to our mutual benefit. It is the fundamentals that matter and not the nonessentials, however desirable they may be. Indians should not think that the United States is anxious to replace the European colonial powers or to build up some other kind of empire. On the other hand, there should be a greater public recognition in the United States of the existence of a democratic regime in India. For that reason alone, India is deserving of much greater support from Americans.

The two spheres in which relations between the United

States and India offer the greatest scope for further development are the economic and the cultural. India has vast resources, human and material, but is as yet underdeveloped. Indians need economic assistance in the form of capital equipment and technical know-how from all those countries which may be in a position to spare them. If the need for development is great, so also are the potentialities. The improvement in the economic well-being of 460 million people is a vast human endeavor. It is in this field that Americans can help us to develop ourselves. Apart from the humanitarian aspect of the question, it is also sound business as well as sound politics to extend such help. India is a very large potential market for all kinds of goods and services but we have to raise the purchasing power of the people before such a market can materialize.

The scope for developing cultural relationship is of course enormous. One has to remember that most of the nationalist movements in Asia in general, and in India in particular, were based on the ideology of the West. These movements were democratic in nature and drew their inspiration from the political thinkers of the West. It is to Rousseau, John Stuart Mill, Herbert Spencer, Emerson and Thoreau that Indian leaders often turned for their guidance. The government and the technique of administration that we see functioning in India, even today, is basically Western, modified no doubt to some extent to suit the genius of our own people. The newspapers, the public associations, the radio and the cinema which have contributed so much in the consolidation of national opinion have come from the West. The rule of law and freedom of thought are other attributes which we share with Western democracies. Continuous cooperation in the cultural field is thus not only possible but is also essential if we are to maintain a mutually profitable relationship. It is in this sphere that Americans can continue to influence and mold the youth of India. Thousands of Indian students are already coming to study in the United States and are taking advantage of the wonderful facilities in American educational institutions. Cultural cooperation will not long remain a one-way traffic. India will soon make valuable contributions of its own, as it did in the past.

To many an American, India still conjures up visions of a land of bejeweled maharajas and naked fakirs, of venomous snakes and snake charmers, of curious customs and the rope trick. I have never seen the rope trick myself; nor have I met anyone who has actually seen it performed. The others, however, do exist, although the maharajas are a fading lot and the snake charmers thrive as tourist attractions. To associate India only with these or to think that this is what the real India is, would of course be absurd. We do not wish either to live in the glories of India's past or to hear only of the seamy side of our life. It is not enough to harp on the abuses of the caste system without saying something about the efforts that are being made to eradicate the evil. It is all very well to describe India as a vast ethnological museum but one must not forget at the same time that India is not merely a distinct geographical unity but has also a cultural and spiritual unity, despite the diversity of its population. We would like to dispel myths with facts. We would prefer to see and hear a good deal more of modern India with the developments that have taken place or are taking place, of our successes and our failures and of our trials and tribulations. An understanding of our tremendous problems and a sympathetic criticism of our failings would always be welcome.

The old relationship between Europe and India, which was based on colonialism, racialism and economic exploitation, must disappear. The new relationship between America and India will have to be based on economic and cultural cooperation even if we have to recognize that complete identity of views on all issues in the political field is not yet achievable. This cooperation will have to be as between brothers without any feeling of domination. We have to learn a great deal from the United States. We shall always continue to be receptive of new ideas and we are keen to acquire all knowledge. We have no desire to retreat to the shell of our old culture. We seek no narrow or aggressive nationalism which might stand in the way of developing an international outlook. At the same time, we will not permit ourselves to be swept off our feet altogether and completely abandon our own culture. We believe that there can be unity in diversity and that a composite culture can be all the richer through a synthesis of different strains of culture. We look forward to an era in which all the different cultural groups of the world irrespective of their race or ideology, while preserving the vital characteristics of their own culture, would cooperate in developing a richer spiritual and moral concept, to the immense benefit of the world as a whole.